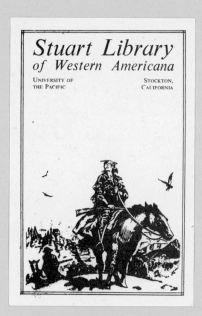

Greg Reynolds

ERNEST MARQUEZ

Ernest Marquez was born in 1924 and grew up in Santa Monica Canyon on what then remained of Rancho Boca de Santa Monica, the Mexican land grant given in 1839 to his great-grandfathers, Francisco Marquez and Ysidro Reyes. In 1942, upon completion of his studies at Santa Monica High School, he enlisted in the U.S. Navy and served for three and a half years in World War II.

After the war he enrolled at the Jefferson Machamer School of Art in Santa Monica and later moved to New York City, where he became a successful free lance cartoonist whose work appeared regularly in the top magazines of those years. During the 1950's, as more and more magazines folded and the cartoon market dwindled steadily, he transferred his talents to the field of commercial art and is today a commercial artist with the Garrett Corporation in Los Angeles.

Aware of his heritage throughout his early life, although not particularly interested in it in those years, he recently became concerned about the many conflicting published versions of his ancestors' role in early California history. He decided to document, using primary research sources rather than published accounts, his family's involvement with California, which began in 1771 when Francisco Reyes came to California as a Spanish soldier to serve in the Monterey Garrison with Father Junipero Serra.

In the course of his project, while gathering data about Santa Monica Canyon in its later years, he developed a fascination for the Long Wharf, "Port Los Angeles," of which this book is the result. In addition to written records, early photographs of Santa Monica and Los Angeles have become an important part of his work and today the Marquez Collection of original photographs and stereoviews is rapidly becoming a valuable and impressive visual history of the area.

:LES

oad Era

All the land visible in this photograph was part
of Rancho Boca de Santa Monica, the Mexican land
grant given to Francisco Marquez and Ysidro Reyes
in 1839. This area was destined to play a major
role in the development of Santa Monica, not only
as a site for a proposed harbor, but later as one
of the most expensive and desirable residential
areas on the Southern California coast.

PORT LOS ANGELES

A Phenomenon of the Railroad Era

by Ernest Marquez

Golden West Books
San Marino, California · 91108

PORT LOS ANGELES

Copyright © 1975 by Ernest Marquez
All Rights Reserved
Published by Golden West Books
San Marino, California 91108 U.S.A.

Library of Congress Catalog Card No. 75-25604
I.S.B.N. 0-87095-060-6

Library of Congress Cataloging in Publication Data

Marquez, Ernest, 1924-
    Port Los Angeles : a phenomenon of the railroad era.

    Bibliography: p.
    Includes index.
    1. Santa Monica, Calif.--Harbor--History.
2. Harbors--California--Los Angeles--History. 3. Rail-
roads--Santa Monica, Calif.--History. I. Title.
HE554.S25M37   387.1'09794'93   75-25604
ISBN 0-87095-060-6

Golden West Books

A Division of Pacific Railroad Publications, Inc.
P.O. BOX 8136 • SAN MARINO, CALIFORNIA • 91108

Dedication
To Mary Eileen, Mary Monica and Ernesto Marquez
in the hope that knowledge and understanding of
the past will ease their way into the future.

Preface

IN THE latter part of the 19th century two major attempts were made to make Santa Monica a significant Southern California commercial seaport. The first effort began in 1875 when Senator John P. Jones of Nevada organized the Los Angeles & Independence Railroad, with its terminus at a wharf in Santa Monica. After a year and a half of operating at a loss, due to a combination of deliberate rate reductions by the Southern Pacific Railroad, lack of support from the people, and losses from other financial investments, Jones was forced to sell his railroad. Collis P. Huntington purchased it, tore down the wharf, and used the Los Angeles to Santa Monica line primarily for excursion trips to the beach. Almost fourteen years later, in 1892, Huntington himself spent over $1,000,000 to build a new wharf, Port Los Angeles, just four miles to the west of the old Los Angeles & Independence wharf.

More than just the building of a wharf was involved in this second instance. Huntington saw an opportunity to obtain a federal government appropriation of $3,098,000 for the development of a deep-water harbor at Santa Monica. Besides, Huntington and his Southern Pacific already had a monopoly. He had secured the right-of-way and, in addition, owned the only wharf, as well as a great deal of the property surrounding it. He used his power and money to influence his "friends" in Washington to see to it that Santa Monica, rather than San Pedro, would be selected by Congress as the site for a deep-water harbor to serve as the official port for the city of Los Angeles.

The account which follows has been compiled by one who is neither scholar by inclination nor writer by trade. An investigation of my family's history has led to, and is for a time almost forcibly eclipsed by, the steady accumulation of material pointing to a broader story. The motivation to set down that story has sprung from my acquisition of illustrations for it.

Overall, this is an attempt to depict a series of events the start of which brought about the founding of Santa Monica, and the end of which saw that city intact and thriving, but not at all what it was intended to be by either of the two national figures who most promoted its development.

The illustrations reproduced in this book came from both private and public collections. The source of each is noted under the individual photo-graph. In every instance I extend my sincerest thanks to the owner or administrator who generously permitted its use.

I also wish to express my thanks to John Haskell Kemble, Ph.D., Professor of History at Pomona College, and to the Reverend Thomas Curry, M.A. Their interest and assistance were invaluable to me in the preparation of the manuscript.

Among others who read the text, I am especially grateful to Ira Swett for his important contributions to its accuracy, and to Donald Duke, whose help and encouragement were major factors in its completion. I am deeply indebted also to Robert Weinstein for permitting me access to his vast collection of photographs, as well as to Victor Plukas of Security Pacific National Bank for the generous supply of photographs from the files of that institution.

Two unique contributors to the work remain to be noted. One is Ray Younghans, whose enthusiasm for Los Angeles' interurban system motivated him to salvage from the trash bins innumerable original records, work orders, and maps of the Pacific Electric Railway. The other is my dear wife Lois, whose command of the typewriter and of the English language must surely be second to none.

Ernest Marquez   March 12, 1975

SANTA MONICA HARBOR
AND SURROUNDINGS

LITH. BRITTON. REY & CO. S.F.

Bancroft Library, Berkeley

Lithograph printed in San Francisco about 1875 by
the firm of Britton and Rey. A tiny train of the
Los Angeles & Independence Railroad is seen
puffing its way toward the first wharf in Santa
Monica, which was the pride of Senator John P.
Jones of Nevada.

Introduction

IT HAS been said that the three requirements for the success of a port are natural endowments, such as protection, depth, and working area ashore; a hinterland with a favorable economic potential; and men of energy and ability eager to promote its growth. Santa Monica, or "Port Los Angeles," possessed only one of these elements in abundance — promoters. John P. Jones and Collis P. Huntington, who had come to California in the Gold Rush and amassed fortunes based on mining and railroading respectively, each undertook to develop a great port on the shores of Santa Monica Bay. They failed largely because the natural qualities of the shoreline simply did not justify a port, and the economic state of the hinterland in their time was still marginal.

Actually, no place on the coast near Los Angeles presented overwhelming advantages as a port location. San Pedro, the original landing for the *pueblo* twenty miles inland, was the best available site, however, and it was not really surprising that it eventually won out in the struggle for federal appropriations and developed into an excellent harbor. Jones and Huntington, though, tried mightily to channel aid in the direction of Santa Monica, and the story of their efforts both in the halls of Congress and in the actual construction of port facilities at Santa Monica is an interesting and important one.

Few of those who today promenade in the pleasant Palisades Park at Santa Monica or who swim and sun themselves at the beaches below Pacific Palisades realize that this was once an area of commercial maritime activity and that two great 19th century tycoons labored long and hard to make it the major port of Southern California. Ernest Marquez brings to this book not only a tradition of family association with the region about which he writes that goes back to the early Spanish period, but also a lifetime of personal knowledge of the area. He has researched the sources carefully and he has a keen sense of the historical and personal drama inherent in the efforts of Jones and Huntington to realize their dreams of a great port on Santa Monica Bay. The story which he tells and the splendid historical photographs which he has collected to accompany it are well worth careful attention.

JOHN HASKELL KEMBLE

Claremont, California

Los Angeles & Independence Railroad Wharf at Santa Monica

" . . . Santa Monica, not Los Angeles, is the
logical metropolitan center of California."
—Senator John P. Jones of Nevada, 1875

Southern Pacific Railroad Wharf at Santa Monica

" . . . I do not find it to my advantage to have
this harbor at San Pedro . . . "
— Collins P. Huntington, 1894

Table of Contents

In 1870 Los Angeles' only railroad was the Los Angeles & San Pedro, a short line built by Phineas Banning. Here, on the right, a Los Angeles & San Pedro mixed train leaves the Wilmington wharf for Los Angeles while, on the left, the side-wheel towboat *Los Angeles* moves away from the dock.

Godfrey Photo 1870.

The Pueblo's Harbor

SAN FRANCISCO and San Diego both have natural landlocked harbors, but there is along the California coastline between these two points, a distance of more than 600 miles, no other natural landlocked harbor. Los Angeles from its earliest beginnings used San Pedro as a port, although it was far from ideal. In 1602 Sebastian Vizcaino, following a course sailed earlier by Juan Rodriguez Cabrillo, came into the bay and named it San Pedro. Later, during the rancho period, ships from New England and even Europe called there regularly to trade with the rancheros for hides and tallow.

San Pedro was the place where Phineas Banning landed when he came to California in 1851. Realizing immediately that potentially it could become a great harbor, he took over an existing wagon trail used by the Californios and developed a stage and wagon line to Los Angeles. He established his base of operations at the inner harbor of San Pedro, away from Timms Landing, and named this spot after his hometown of Wilmington, Delaware. Banning's efforts also brought about the construction in 1869 of Los Angeles' first rail line, the Los Angeles & San Pedro Railroad, along his wagon trail route.

San Pedro continued to serve as the pueblo's "harbor," even as it became obvious that vessels drawing more than 17 feet of water could not enter. Extensive dredging and breakwater installations would be necessary to develop the harbor properly. Financing a project of such magnitude was far beyond the capacity of so young a city.

By 1872 it had become apparent that if Los Angeles was to develop into a major metropolis it must have an outside connection by railroad as well as by port. The Southern Pacific Railroad was already laying track southward from San Francisco toward Yuma, Arizona. Los Angeles was not included in the road's initial plans. The officials of the Southern Pacific did not consider the pueblo important enough to build 150 miles of additional track to reach it, let alone to make it a terminal point.

Realizing the disastrous effect of being by-passed, the city officials of Los Angeles met with the railroad leaders, and the Southern Pacific named its price for bringing the railroad to Los Angeles. The agreement included a sum of $600,000, representing five per cent of the total assessed valuation of the County of Los Angeles, a right-of-way 25 feet wide, 60 acres of land for depot purposes, and the existing Los Angeles & San Pedro Railroad. (The Banning family was not desirous of giving up the Los Angeles & San Pedro, but the city held most of its bonds. Thus they were forced to sell the road to the municipality.)

The total proposition was agreed to by the voters in November 1872, and the Southern Pacific Railroad, now owner of the Los Angeles to San Pedro standard gauge line, assumed a position of virtual control over all shipping to and from Los Angeles. In fact, the Southern Pacific had no competition at any seaport along the entire Southern California coast.

Robert Weinstein Collection

2

Collis P. Huntington and the Southern Pacific were now becoming a powerful force in the city. Many considered the two to be a single entity, for Huntington's primary motivation was always the welfare of the Southern Pacific, which he thought of as his own, and in whose interest he would go to any extreme.

In his book *Citizen Hearst,* a lengthy biography of the newspaper magnate who early on levelled his publications' guns at Huntington, W. A. Swanberg writes: "The power behind the Southern Pacific was huge, Yankee-born Collis P. Huntington, a miserly millionaire who had been a gold-rush hardware dealer in Sacramento with a genius for cornering the supply of such necessities as nails or shovels and then charging all the traffic would bear. Later branching into railroad building with the aid of stupendous government grants, he had cornered transportation and followed the same policy."

In the next few years prices for hauling goods by rail to San Pedro grew more and more prohibitive, despite public complaints and protest meetings. Thus when Senator John P. Jones of Nevada announced in 1875 that he intended to build a railroad from Santa Monica, via Los Angeles through Cajon Pass and Mojave, to Independence in Inyo County and then on to Salt Lake to eventually connect with a transcontinental line, the news was greeted with great enthusiasm. It was hoped that the resultant competition in the Los Angeles area would help break Huntington's stranglehold on the city's commerce.

San Pedro before the advent of the railroad. Ships anchored offshore and cargoes were brought to land on boats and then transported to Los Angeles by horse and wagon.

Santa Monica

JOHN P. JONES was born in 1829 in Hereford County, England. While still an infant he was brought to the United States by his parents, who settled in Cleveland, Ohio. In 1850 young Jones came to California to prospect, and later became a supervisor at the Crown Point Mine of the Comstock Lode in Virginia City, Nevada. He did well there and purchased large quantities of stock in the mine at a period when its value had depreciated to $2.00 per share. Subsequently there was a bonanza and the mine yielded $6,000,000, one-half of which went to its stockholders. Overnight, Jones was making more than $1,000,000 a year, not only off the Comstock Lode but also from other financial investments, which included a part interest in the Panamint Silver Mines in Inyo County, California.

The Panamint operations were near the town of Independence and Jones, with an eye to controlling all freight moving in and out of the region, decided to build a railroad that would extend from Independence to Santa Monica Bay, an exclusive outlet to the sea. As it turned out, however, he actually started building the line from the road's destination rather than from the mines.

The Bay of Santa Monica does not actually constitute a harbor in the strict sense of the word, since it is quite open to the ocean. It was believed, however, that because of the formation of the land at either end it was for the greatest part of the year as safe as any landlocked harbor. Moreover a terminus there would present an advantage to Los

Angeles shippers over a port at San Pedro, because Santa Monica was four miles nearer to Los Angeles and one and one-half hours closer by steamer to San Francisco.

In December 1874 the Senator came to Santa Monica with a party of associates, including surveyors. His escort was Colonel Robert Baker, a man whose recent investments in land in the Santa Monica area had spanned a considerable amount of territory. In 1872, for $55,000, Baker had bought the 38,409-acre Rancho San Vicente from the heirs of Francisco Sepulveda. In 1873 he had purchased 2,112 acres of Rancho Boca de Santa Monica (in the form of an undivided one-half interest in that rancho), for which he had paid $6,000 to Maria Antonia Reyes, widow of Ysidro Reyes. In addition he held a one-half interest in part of Rancho La Ballona, just to the south of Rancho San Vicente, a grant owned by the brothers Agustín and Ygnacio Machado together with José Tomas Talamantez.

Shortly after Senator Jones' visit came the announcement that he had purchased from Colonel Baker, for $162,500, a three-quarter interest in the latter's land holdings, and that Baker had become an officer of the proposed Los Angeles & Independence Railroad.

Within the next month Jones laid out a town, registered it as the Township of Santa Monica, and began development of his railroad. It was chartered on January 7, 1875, with a capital stock of $4,-000,000. Its directors were Senator Jones, President; Colonel Baker, Francis Temple, Trenor W.

An artist's conception of Santa Monica in 1876. By that time its population had grown to about 1,000. It was believed by the promoters of Santa Monica and the Los Angeles & Independence Railroad that the formation of the mountains and the shape of the bay made Santa Monica an ideal location for a harbor. The Los Angeles & Independence tracks and wharf were built in 1875, and their actual arrangement was somewhat different from the way the artist has depicted it.

5

Park, Johnathan S. Slauson; James A. Prichard, Secretary; and Joseph Crawford, Chief Engineer. The first section to be built was the line from Santa Monica to Los Angeles. Plans called for it to be extended eventually to Independence and ultimately on to Nevada and Salt Lake.

Although the existence of such a railroad, together with a wharf at Santa Monica, would pose an obvious threat to the Southern Pacific's commercial monopoly principally at San Pedro, officials of the Southern Pacific did little at this point to impede Jones' activity. Huntington, concentrating on bringing the Southern Pacific's tracks from San Francisco to Los Angeles, merely commented that

In 1869 John P. Jones of Nevada became one of the richest men in the West, by way of his interests in the silver mines on the Comstock Lode. He was extremely popular among Nevadans for his heroism in saving the lives of miners in the Yellow Jacket mine fire, and for his subsequent kindness and planning for the families who lost relatives in the disaster. He shared his fortune with his friends by buying for them, with his own money, shares in the Crown Point Mine. Taking advantage of this popularity, he ran for the U.S. Senate, was elected in 1872, and continued to hold that office for 30 years.

Robert S. Baker was born in Providence, Rhode Island in 1825. Although he joined the Gold Rush in 1849, he actually made his fortune in the sheep and cattle trades. In 1872 he purchased Rancho San Vicente, as well as a one-half undivided interest in Rancho Boca de Santa Monica. In 1875 Baker married Dona Arcadia Bandini de Stearns, the widow of Don Abel Stearns, a man who at one time owned more acreage in Southern California than any person before or since. Upon Stearns' death in 1871 his widow had acquired the bulk of his estate. After their marriage Baker and Arcadia resided at *El Palacio* on Main Street in Los Angeles, the home Stearns had built some 30 years before. In 1877, however, that famous mansion was torn down to make way for the Baker Block, said to have been financed with Arcadia's money. Baker deeded one-third of all his unsold real estate in Santa Monica to Arcadia as her separate property (hardly a gift, since she paid him $50,000 for it). Colonel Robert Baker died in 1894.

Security Pacific National Bank

The Los Angeles & Independence wharf under construction. Railroad ties and lumber, brought to Santa Monica on ships seen docked alongside, are stacked upon the wharf ready for hauling to the track construction site as the railroad makes its way toward Los Angeles.

Two steamships from San Francisco brought prospective buyers to Santa Monica for the land auction. The above advertisement appeared as a half-page ad on the front page of the San Francisco theatrical newspaper *Figaro* on Friday, July 9, 1875.

he was sure in the end Jones would be hurt more than he, a prediction which proved accurate.

By February 1875 construction of the Los Angeles & Independence Railroad was under way. The wharf had to be erected first and to extend far enough out to sea so that ships carrying rails, ties, and other supplies and equipment for use in building the first section of the line could dock. All material was to be carried by ship rather than by rail because the Los Angeles & Independence was to be in no way dependent upon the Southern Pacific.

The wharf, completed by May 1875, was 1,740 feet long and 80 feet wide at its ocean end, where there was a warehouse and a depot and where water depth at low tide was 24 feet, sufficient for ocean steamers. A track curved from the wharf to the railroad yards, which lay south of it.

Grading for the tracks began at the same time as construction of the wharf. According to the *Los Angeles Herald,* 100 Chinese were brought down from San Francisco for the job. Track laying from the wharf began August 31, 1875, and in early September a sidewheel steamer delivered the first engine, along with flat cars and gondolas. The

equipment was set up and pulling a construction train by September 26. The train hauled rails, ties, and other supplies to the construction site at the end of the track as it progressed toward Los Angeles, a total rail distance of 18.53 miles from Santa Monica.

Advertisements promoting the proposed new town and seaport appeared in July 1875 newspapers throughout the State as well as in other parts of the nation. By wagon from Los Angeles and by special ship from San Francisco potential buyers came to attend a great land auction.

Indeed, even before the construction of the railroad, Santa Monica had begun to take on the image of a successful and popular summer resort. Campers were spending weekends in tents along the beach or under the sycamore trees in Santa Monica Canyon where the Marquez and Reyes families welcomed visitors with true Californio hospitality, supplying them with food and fresh milk from cows kept on their ranch. (Francisco Marquez and Ysidro Reyes had settled in this area long before 1839, the year in which Rancho Boca de Santa Monica was officially granted to them by the Mexican government. Their land grant extended from a point just above Topanga Canyon south along the ocean to an indentation in the cliffs below Santa Monica Canyon, then east to a point near Mandeville Canyon, then west to Fernwood in Topanga Canyon, then down to the point of beginning. Considered a small rancho in those days, it represented a total of 6,656 acres.)

In 1875 Santa Monica Canyon was a popular spot for visitors to the beach. Swimmers, picnickers, and campers came to the Canyon by stage from Los Angeles, and the Marquez and Reyes families, owners of the area, not only welcomed them, but encouraged them to stay as long as they liked. As early as the 1860's even, tent saloons were set up — usually from June until September.

The Los Angeles & Independence wharf at Santa
Monica, completed in May 1875, was 1,740 feet
long and 80 feet wide. Tracks curving to the
left lead to the railroad's yards just to the
south of the wharf, then loop around and
connect to the main line back to Los Angeles.

On October 17, 1875, less than a year after Senator Jones' visit to Santa Monica with Colonel Baker, the first train of the Los Angeles & Independence Railroad made its maiden run, although at the time track had been laid only as far as La Cienega. For Jones and the citizens of Santa Monica it was a triumphal occasion. It was also a highly visible event, because the railroad's passenger cars had not yet arrived and the travelers sat on chairs on the beds of flat cars roofed over with awnings. The train started from the Cienega Station in the morning and ran to Santa Monica over unballasted roadbed, a distance of 10 miles. A crowd cheered the departing train and just 19 minutes later another crowd enthusiastically welcomed it at the Santa Monica wharf.

The Los Angeles & Independence depot in Los Angeles was located on San Pedro Street near Wolfskill Lane (Fourth Street). It was an imposing structure with twin towers, made even more impressive by twin bronze sphinxes crouching one on either side of its broad steps. On November 31, 1875, when the last spike was driven in front of the depot, the Southern Pacific reacted. It announced that effective immediately its rates for shipments from Los Angeles to San Pedro would be reduced by half. The new station opened and regular service began on December 1, whereupon the Southern Pacific announced a further reduction in its rates for fares and freight. The hopes of shippers and consumers were raised, for it seemed that competition was indeed going to have an effect on the Southern Pacific's excessive rates.

Senator Jones was not unduly concerned about the Southern Pacific's tactics. He was in good financial shape and prepared to wait awhile for profits. Moreover, by way of his position in the Senate, he was planning to block any further appropriations for the harbor at San Pedro and at the same time achieve passage of an appropriation for a breakwater at Santa Monica. He openly declared that he would "ruin Wilmington," and that Santa Monica, not Los Angeles, was the "logical metropolitan center of California."

Meanwhile, rivalry between the two "ports" was leading to great public confusion. Passengers board-

The Los Angeles & Independence train at the depot in Los Angeles. Passengers and crew stop to pose before making the 18-mile trip to Santa Monica.

Looking east from a point near Third and Olive Streets about 1876 (Third Street in foreground). "The Round House," with pointed roof, stood on Main Street. It was an attraction to which visitors came to view its gardens, and was later used as a school. Twin towers of the Los Angeles & Independence Railroad Station can be seen in the distance at right.

Ernest Marquez Collection

View down San Pedro Street towards Second Street from one of the towers of the Los Angeles & Independence depot. The tracks terminated at the wharf in Santa Monica.

The Los Angeles & Independence Railroad depot was built on San Pedro Street near Wolfskill Lane (Fourth Street) after many long, bitter arguments among city legislators over where it should be located. Some suggested the Plaza be leased to the railroad; others favored the Aliso Street Tract as the site. Finally, in September 1875, an ordinance was passed which granted the railroad a franchise to operate along city streets to a depot site on San Pedro Street.

Robert Weinstein Collection

Ernest Marquez Collection

13

ing ship for Los Angeles from San Francisco found themselves unable to ascertain in advance whether their ship would dock at Santa Monica or San Pedro. The decision often depended upon whether the Captain's sympathies lay with Huntington or with Jones, or upon which port represented the greater financial advantage under the particular circumstances. Southern Californians themselves were equally uncertain as to the direction in which they should head to meet arrivals from the north. A journey from one port to the other was difficult and required a day's time. Freight rates were cheap, but inconveniences and annoyances were mounting. Shipping lines began to be subjected to strong influence by the Southern Pacific to use San Pedro, and those lines which depended on that railroad for their business yielded to Huntington's pressures.

By December 19, 1875 a second engine for the Los Angeles & Independence had arrived, and an additional coach was delivered on January 15, 1876. A third coach was put into service on January 18, and a fourth by January 30. All rolling stock was built by the Wason Manufacturing Company of Springfield, Massachusetts, and shipped around the Horn to avoid a haul over the Central Pacific to Oakland and transfer there to a ship bound for Santa Monica. On March 8, 1876 Senator Jones' luxurious parlor car, built by the Kimball Manufacturing Company of San Francisco, made its appearance. It contained two drawing rooms upholstered in crimson velvet, one equipped with berths, and passengers who rode in it paid 50 cents extra fare for the privilege.

"Gala excursions" between Los Angeles and Santa Monica continued to be a great success. By 1876 two trains a day were making the round trip. The fare was $1.00 per person, and the schedule was planned so that excursionists could spend fully five hours bathing, fishing, or picnicking on the beach.

Nevertheless, the picture was darkening for the Los Angeles & Independence as the impact of Southern Pacific rate cutting made itself felt. On May 21, 1876 the *San Francisco Chronicle* published figures indicating that Wilmington was handling twice as much business as Santa Monica. In September the Southern Pacific completed its line from San Francisco to Los Angeles. Freight

Security Pacific National Bank

14

By January 1876 the second engine and a supply of shiny new rolling stock had arrived by ship from the East coast around the Horn. Senator John P. Jones, second from right, and an unidentified group pose in front of the passenger cars.

Southern Pacific Company

The depot and freight house at the end of the
Los Angeles & Independence wharf. Steamship
docked alongside has discharged passengers,
who are purchasing tickets for the train
ride to Los Angeles.

coming into Southern California at Santa Monica could be hauled only as far as Los Angeles, whereas freight coming in at San Pedro could be "long-hauled" to other points on the Southern Pacific line, a benefit with which the Los Angeles & Independence could not compete.

Jones could not keep his railroad running at a loss indefinitely. Gradually, service on the Los Angeles & Independence deteriorated, thus by default losing for Santa Monica the influx of businessmen from Los Angeles who might have built their summer homes in the new town, given a regular and reliable means of transportation to and from the city.

Late in August 1875 financial panic in Comstock securities had caused the Bank of California in San Francisco to close its doors. Los Angeles banks were hit by the panic that ensued, and a run on the Los Angeles bank of Workman and Temple brought it down. A final crash occurred in Janu-

Los Angeles & Independence Engine No. 1 was brought to Santa Monica from the East coast around the Horn by sidewheel steamer and unloaded at the wharf. It was then used to transport the ties and rails, as they arrived by ship, from the wharf to the current construction area on the route from Santa Monica to Los Angeles along which track was being laid.

Los Angeles County Museum of Natural History

17

Los Angeles County Museum of Natural History

Panorama of Santa Monica from the Los Angeles &
Independence wharf, with roofs of railroad cars
in the foreground. On top of the bluff to the
north of the wharf stands the Santa Monica
Hotel with its four chimneys, Santa Monica's

Ernest Marquez Collection

first such hostelry. On the beach below is the
Santa Monica Bath House, built for tourists who
came by train to Santa Monica to swim or picnic
on the beach. On the south side of the wharf
are the railroad's storage areas and warehouse.

19

View from the balcony of the Santa Monica Hotel. On the left is the Pavilion, where tourists could purchase refreshments. At far right, a shelter with benches and tables overlooks the wharf and the Santa Monica Bath House on the beach below.

Santa Monica's first hotel, built in 1875 at Ocean Avenue and Colorado Boulevard. It advertised as "a first class hotel in every respect, with open fireplace in every room." The entire structure except for the fireplace chimneys burned to the ground in 1889.

Ernest Marquez Collection

Melzer Lindsey Collection

21

ary 1876, and depression swept the State. Jones lost all his local financial support. It was known that the Panamint Mines had failed and that a number of his other investments had become losing propositions. Surveying and construction of the railroad beyond Los Angeles were halted, and rumors spread that Jones was looking for a buyer.

Early in 1877 Jones and the other directors of the Los Angeles & Independence acknowledged their inability to compete with the Southern Pacific, and offered to sell their railroad at cost to the County of Los Angeles. The County refused the offer for fear of incurring the displeasure of the Southern Pacific, whose power in the State was already close to absolute. Jones then approached Jay Gould, the head of the Union Pacific Railroad. Unbeknownst to the Senator, however, Collis Hunt-

In the spring of 1876, according to figures published in the *San Francisco Chronicle* on May 21 of that year, Wilmington was still doing twice as much business as Santa Monica. The newspaper reported the following statistics for the month from March 14 to April 14:

Steamers arriving at Wilmington:	**12**
Steamers arriving at Santa Monica:	**6**
Passengers arriving at Wilmington:	**634**
Passengers arriving at Santa Monica:	**345**
Freight exported from Wilmington:	**1,712 tons**
Freight exported from Santa Monica:	**311 tons**
Freight unloaded from Wilmington:	**3,232 tons**
Freight unloaded from Santa Monica:	**1,003 tons**

The Santa Monica Bath House (later called the North Beach Bath House) was located on the north side of the wharf. Built to accommodate visitors to the beach, it featured an indoor, heated, saltwater swimming pool, to which the windmill on the right pumped water from the ocean. The tent beside the boardwalk was originally the studio of E. G. Morrison, an early photographer of Santa Monica. Later it became the studio of H. F. Rile, who photographed Santa Monica extensively for many years.

ington had already convinced Gould that the Los Angeles & Independence would be a poor investment and he backed away.

Jones, who was now out of funds and desperate, had no alternative but to offer to sell his railroad to the Southern Pacific. Officials of the Southern Pacific urged Huntington not to buy it. Their argument was that such an act would only provide more ammunition to those who were already charging "monopoly." Huntington did not share their concern. He wanted to keep the Nevada legislator friendly in view of his influence in the United States Senate. Nevertheless, Jones, who had $1,000,000 invested in the little railroad, received only $250,000 from its sale.

Some optimistic citizens thought selling the failing Los Angeles & Independence to the Southern Pacific was a good idea, on the theory that the bigger railroad would make needed improvements and Santa Monica would thus continue to develop into a major seaport.

The formal transfer of the Los Angeles & Independence to the Southern Pacific took place on

Robert Weinstein Collection

23

June 4, 1877, whereupon the Southern Pacific promptly *raised* its rates on the Los Angeles to San Pedro run to figures *higher than any previous transportation charges*.

When the Los Angeles & Independence tracks were connected to those of the Southern Pacific, the depot of the former was no longer used and the Southern Pacific sold the station. Thereafter, two trains per day ran to and from Santa Monica, leaving the Southern Pacific's River Station at 9:30 A.M. and 4:20 P.M., with an extra train on Sundays. The four Wason cars remained in service, but Senator Jones' parlor car disappeared. Presumably, the Southern Pacific sold it. (The Los Angeles & Independence depot was leased by its new owner to the California Door Company and loaded with $100,000 worth of door-manufacturing equipment. On October 30, 1888 it caught fire and burned to the ground. The two crouching sphinxes which had adorned its entrance were purchased by a Cora Phillips and decorated her brothel on Alameda Street for many years.)

The last steamer to dock at Santa Monica was, ironically enough, the *Senator* (Pacific Coast Steamship Company), which arrived in September 1878. After that the port's name was removed from coastal shipping lists. In the same month the Southern Pacific dispatched a team of engineers to Santa Monica to examine the wharf. They reported that it was unsafe, that it was infested with sea worms (microscopic animals less than one-sixteenth of an inch in diameter called "teredos"), and that to prevent its imminent collapse three-fourths of the piles should be replaced.

The Southern Pacific concluded that such extensive repairs would be too costly, and decided instead to abandon and dismantle the wharf. On January 2, 1879 work began on tearing it down. In spite of the engineers' report that the piles were almost eaten through, the workmen sent to demolish the wharf had a good deal of difficulty in doing so and ultimately had to saw the piles off at the waterline during low tide.

A pervasive gloom now settled over Santa Monica, and the town went into a "slump." Business failures were common, property values sank, and within a few months the population had dropped from 1,000 to 350 citizens. Thus, in a little over a year, Collis P. Huntington had literally eradicated the threat to his Southern Pacific's monopoly of Los Angeles shipping, and nearly destroyed a town as well.

After the Southern Pacific tore down the Los
Angeles & Independence wharf, a lonely stub
was left, useful for nothing more than a fishing
pier. A vivid reminder of the real reason for
the founding of Santa Monica — to provide a sea
terminus for a railroad which its planners hoped
would ultimately span the continent — it was still
standing as late as 1909, when a new pier, made
of cement, was built at the same location.

Melzer Lindsey Collection

25

San Pedro

A S FOR San Pedro, over the years from 1871 to 1892 it received from the federal government a total of $954,000 in appropriations for development of and improvements to its inner harbor. A jetty was built to join Rattlesnake Island to Deadman's Island. (Rattlesnake Island derived its name from the fact that rattlesnakes were found there periodically, believed by early settlers to have been washed down from inland regions during flood periods. After the Dominguez family sold the tract to the Terminal Land Company in 1892 it was known as Terminal Island.) This closed the ebb and flow of the tide to the various channels between them, thus forcing all the water out the west side of Deadman's Island which resulted in a natural scouring of the main channel. The main channel itself was straightened, widened, and deepened. The amounts of the individual appropriations were so small, however, that it was impossible to keep up with the deterioration and destruction brought about by Nature alone.

With the onset of a boom in the 1880's, San Pedro's rickety piers and outmoded facilities posed a pressing problem. Extensive development was imperative to handle the steady increase in traffic, and Los Angeles civic leaders agreed that a major effort should be made to complete the inner harbor there.

Looming over their attempts to move ahead, however, was the figure of Collis P. Huntington and his omnipresent Southern Pacific. By this time the Southern Pacific was charging more to move freight from Los Angeles to San Pedro than it cost to move the cargo from San Pedro to Hong Kong. Shippers were completely at the mercy of his railroad. There wasn't any other way for shippers to get their products to or from the harbor. The Southern Pacific enjoyed maximum freedom from competition and was therefore free to adopt a system of freight rates which reflected the highest charge the traffic would bear without completely bankrupting the shipper and thus eliminating future business. The railroad could favor one and ruin another by quoting them differing rates for the same service. Often an agent would demand to see a shipper's books, and then set the rate at what he thought the latter could afford.

The railroad also developed its great power politically, as well as through its manipulation of freight rates. It could reward its friends and punish its enemies. If a politician did not have economic interests of his own that could be favored or ruined by rate changing, his constituents did. Huntington's ability to influence lawmakers at all levels of government took on an assortment of disguises. If the legislator happened to be a lawyer, he might receive a check for unspecified "legal services." Otherwise, there were contributions for "campaign expenses." The Southern Pacific had developed a political machine far more powerful than any other in the State, and California's government as well as its economy had become a prisoner of the railroad.

The citizens of Los Angeles grew more and more indignant over this state of affairs. They held mass

In 1881 the Southern Pacific extended the Los Angeles & San Pedro Railroad across the Wilmington Lagoon to this point near Timms' Landing

Robert Weinstein Collection

Robert Weinstein Collection

28

In the late 1870's ships arrived daily at San Pedro with large supplies of lumber destined for use in the construction of buildings and homes in the fast-growing *pueblo* of Los Angeles.

meetings, implored the State legislature to pass a rate regulation bill, and sent representatives to Washington. All this was to no avail in the face of Huntington's ability to influence lawmakers from all parts of the nation. Unmoved by their increasing outrage, he now extended his hold over Los Angeles harbor commerce by purchasing a right-of-way along the east basin frontage of San Pedro and various other sections of the shoreline as far north as and including Santa Monica.

In 1888 the Los Angeles Chamber of Commerce was formed to foster trade. In order to bring foreign commerce to the area, a deep-water harbor was a necessity. Accordingly, the new Chamber made this its number one project. San Pedro was considered to be the natural site for such a deep-water harbor, and it was thought that a stone sea wall or breakwater about two miles in length, constructed from a point a little north of Point Fermin, would accomplish the objective. The cost of such a structure was estimated as somewhere between $4,000,000 and $5,000,000.

The Chamber was not too optimistic about getting such a large appropriation. At the time, it felt that because development of the inner harbor at San Pedro was still incomplete, the government was unlikely to institute a new project in the same area. To make matters worse, the numbers and amounts of appropriations for river and harbor bills had been increasing steadily over the years and a general outcry against "extravagance" was arising throughout the nation. The cost of construction of a deep-water harbor was enormous, and Congress would be bound to think twice about it. In spite of the discouraging outlook, however, the Chamber did set out to obtain some funds: first, enough to finish the inner harbor; second, a small amount to prepare for a deepwater harbor.

One of the methods used by the Los Angeles Chamber of Commerce to promote its endeavors on behalf of the harbor was to take Senators, Congressmen, and other well-known or influential persons who visited the area to San Pedro on a special train supplied free of charge by the Southern Pacific. Enthusiastic and articulate harbor advocates would describe to the visitors the feasibility and advantages of a breakwater there. In October 1889 probably the most important figure to be con-

29

cerned with the subject came to Los Angeles, Senator William B. Frye of Maine, Chairman of the Senate Commerce Committee. In any case of monetary appropriations by the government for the development of harbors he had a tight hold on the purse strings, and Frye was at that time touring the United States to inspect various such projects on which his committee would be voting.

Frye and the fellow committee members who were accompanying him on the junket were, of course, escorted on the grand tour to San Pedro. With them went an impressive party which included Major E. W. Jones, President of the Los Angeles Chamber of Commerce; Dr. J. P. Widney, Chairman of the Chamber committee responsible for the harbor project; Leland Stanford, then President of the Southern Pacific Railroad; and some 30 members of the Chamber, armed with charts, maps,

San Pedro looked much like this in 1889 when Senator Frye, Chairman of the Senate Commerce Committee, escorted by Los Angeles Chamber of Commerce officials, came to inspect it. Group would have passed through this area on its way to Timms' Point.

Robert Weinstein Collection

30

and statistics anent the proposed development.

It was on this occasion that Senator Frye by his remarks astonished and infuriated not only his escorts, but the general citizenry of Los Angeles as well. When the special train reached the end of the Southern Pacific's line, which ran out to a site beyond Timms Point where the company was in the process of building a new wharf, the party left the cars. Senator Frye looked over the harbor and saw a few ships anchored in the windy and badly exposed area surrounded by mud flats, sand hills, and dank sloughs. He turned to his hosts and said, "Well, as near as I can make out you propose to ask the government to create a harbor for you, almost out of whole cloth. The Lord has not given you much to start with, that is certain. It will cost four or five millions to build, you say. Well, is your whole country worth that much?"

"It seems," the Senator continued, "you made a big mistake in the location of your city. You should have put it at some point where a harbor already exists, instead of calling upon the government to give you what Nature refused." He concluded by suggesting they move the city to San Diego, where a good harbor already existed.

The next day, the newspapers in both Los Angeles and San Diego made headlines of Frye's comments. Hopes for a deep-water harbor at San Pedro seemed shattered. Frye himself later told reporters that the Los Angeles citizens shouldn't have taken his remarks so seriously, that he had intended them to be jocular. On the very day they made the front pages, however, the Senator, who on this sojourn to Southern California was the guest of Senator Jones at the latter's home in Santa Monica, stood on the cliff overlooking Santa Monica Bay and further allowed that *that* was the spot for a port. In view of what was to come, that would seem to have been somewhat more than a "passing comment."

An 1887 advertisement announced that Port Ballona "is the future harbor for Southern California on account of its location and facilities and will command a large proportion of the commerce of China, Japan, and the Islands of the Pacific Ocean destined for Los Angeles, Chicago, New York, and the great cities of the North."

For in these last years of the 1880's the Southern Pacific's hold over shipping in the Los Angeles area did seem to be weakening somewhat. In 1887 the Atchison, Topeka & Santa Fe Railroad had sought an ocean terminal. Since frontage at San Pedro, Wilmington, and Santa Monica was part of the domain of Huntington and the Southern Pacific and obviously not open to any other railroad, Moses L. Wicks, a lawyer and land developer who had control of some of the Rancho La Ballona property, interested the Atchison, Topeka & Santa Fe in a potential harbor at the Ballona Lagoon, just south of Santa Monica (at the present Marina del Rey). Plans for the harbor had been drawn up and the Atchison, Topeka & Santa Fe actually laid track from Los Angeles to the site, but the entire venture failed when a land boom collapsed and potential customers for the line failed to materialize.

Then, in 1889, the Redondo Railway Company was organized. It constructed a wharf at Redondo and built a narrow-gauge railroad from there to Los Angeles. Redondo, located about midway between San Pedro and Santa Monica, offered an advantage

A view from the Redondo Hotel of shipping at the Redondo facility about 1890. Left to right: barkentine *Katie Flickinger;* steamer *Corona;* steamer *Cabrillo;* steamer *Santa Rosa* (at the pier). In front of the *Santa Rosa* is the Southern Pacific tug *Collis.* On the offshore side of the wharf is a five-masted East Coast schooner, the *Governor Ames.*

By the late 1880's Redondo was one of the Santa Fe Railroad's Pacific ports. Docked at the wharf is a Pacific Coast Steamship Company vessel.

Ernest Marquez Collection

34

By 1892 Redondo posed a serious threat to the Southern Pacific Railroad's monopoly at San Pedro. Redondo was preferred because ships could tie up alongside the wharf and unload cargo and passengers directly onto railroad cars, thus saving considerable time and money. The Redondo Hotel on the left, opened in 1890, was a luxury installation and a landmark for many years.

over San Pedro. A natural deep canyon in the ocean in front of it made it possible for only a short wharf to reach deep water. This meant that deep-draft vessels, which had previously had to anchor at San Pedro and unload their cargoes onto lighters, could tie up at the Redondo wharf and unload there directly, thus saving both time and expense. Later that same year the Atchison, Topeka & Santa Fe, still seeking an ocean terminal, built southward from a junction with its abandoned Ballona line and constructed a second wharf at Redondo. Soon great quantities of freight from the north were arriving in Los Angeles by way of these installations rather than via San Pedro.

Indeed, the steady increase from 1890 to 1892 in the number of ships stopping at Redondo resulted in that port's handling over 60 per cent of the water traffic in and out of Los Angeles exclusive of shipments of coal and lumber. Coal and cut lumber were primarily for the use of the Southern Pacific itself and continued to be handled at San Pedro.

Still another development of ominous portent to the Southern Pacific was the acquisition by the Terminal Land Company of Rattlesnake Island in the inner harbor area of San Pedro. It was known that this foothold was being reserved to serve as an ocean terminus either for the Union Pacific or for some other railroad planning to build westward to the coast.

Huntington, realizing that he could not dominate forever at San Pedro, and that Redondo was posing a more and more serious threat, now began to prepare for a move that would ultimately bring on a long and bitter battle involving not only the people of Los Angeles and of Santa Monica, but legislators in Washington and even the President of the United States. For Huntington had decided that the only way to insure control of shipping for the Southern Pacific was to have his own harbor, at Santa Monica. Of course this plan was to be kept under wraps until the groundwork for its accomplishment had been properly laid.

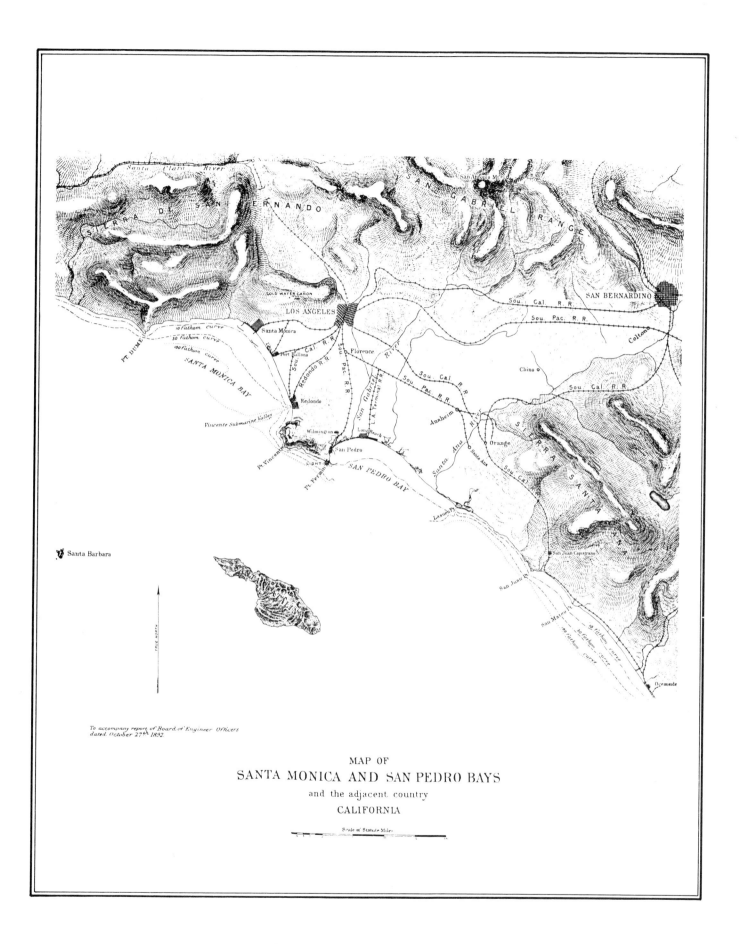

MAP OF
SANTA MONICA AND SAN PEDRO BAYS
and the adjacent country
CALIFORNIA

Scale of Statute Miles

37

Collis P. Huntington, the power behind the Southern Pacific Railroad.

Port Los Angeles

ON APRIL 9, 1890 a change occurred in the management of the Southern Pacific. Leland Stanford, long an advocate of San Pedro for a deep-water harbor, was suddenly and unexpectedly deposed, and Collis Huntington took over as President. Once in complete control of the company, the latter moved with haste to firm up his plans for Santa Monica. He applied for a wharf franchise, putting up a $5,000 bond, purchased a one-half interest in Senator Jones' land holdings at Santa Monica for $125,000, and employed a number of agents to buy up still more land in the vicinity.

The spring of 1890 also saw Congress approve an appropriation of $5,000 to cover the expense of preparing a project for a deep-water harbor somewhere in the vicinity of Los Angeles. The Act did not specify exactly where such a harbor was to be located, only that the site should be between Point Dume and Capistrano. In this connection a three-man War Department Board of Engineers, headed by Colonel G. H. Mendell, held hearings in San Pedro, Los Angeles, and Santa Monica. All possible sites between Point Dume and Capistrano were discussed, and all except San Pedro and Santa Monica were rejected.

There was no great local publicity about these hearings by the Mendell Board because it was generally assumed that San Pedro would be selected. As it turned out, most of the discussion at these meetings centered around the advantages of Santa Monica. A breakwater to be placed directly in front of that town was proposed and considered. It would be 8,250 feet long and cover an anchorage ground between Point Dume and Rocky Point. The westerly 2,000 feet of the sea wall would be in water seven and one-half to nine fathoms deep, and the remainder in water eight and nine fathoms deep. To construct it of rubble and concrete would cost an estimated $5,715,965.

Nevertheless, the general assumption proved to be correct. In its final report, which was submitted to Congress on December 9, 1891, the Mendell Board recommended San Pedro as the better location, summing up its findings as follows:

> In view of the fact that San Pedro Bay in its natural condition affords better protection both from prevailing winds and from dangerous storms than Santa Monica Bay; that protection can be secured at less cost for equal development of breakwater at the former than at the latter; that larger area of protected anchorage from the prevailing westerly swells can be secured, the severe storms from the southwest being infrequent; and that there is already an interior harbor that will be a valuable addition to an outer harbor; the Board considers San Pedro Bay as the better location for the deep-water harbor provided for by the Act.

The Los Angeles Chamber of Commerce quickly urged Congress to implement the project without delay.

Even while the Board had been deliberating, Collis Huntington had continued to further his interests in Santa Monica. On July 23, 1891 Bonifacio and Pascual Marquez, owners of the beach frontage at Santa Monica Canyon, entered into an agreement with a subsidiary of the Southern Pacific known as the Pacific Improvement Company granting the latter a right-of-way for the laying of tracks across a strip of their property 200 feet long and 100 feet wide, bordering the ocean. Consideration for this easement was the payment of $1 plus the benefits to be derived by its owners from the construction and operation of a railroad between the city of Los Angeles and the Southern Pacific's wharf. In his overall plan Huntington even included an estate, complete with mansion, overlooking his new domain. As the site for it he purchased from Abbot Kinney, who had previously acquired them from

Francisca Marquez de Peña, the sister of Bonifacio and Pascual Marquez, 249 acres, including several hundred feet of ocean frontage, on the north side of Santa Monica Canyon. Within weeks a group of Southern Pacific surveyors made camp in the Canyon and began surveying and mapping.

The Southern Pacific now announced that just north of Santa Monica Canyon it was going to build a gigantic wharf which would extend almost a mile out into the ocean. Citizens of Santa Monica proper were at first disappointed that the location was to be so far north of their city; but as soon as they realized the magnitude of the project, they accepted the enterprise as their own.

On July 23, 1891 the brothers Bonifacio and Pascual Marquez entered into an agreement with the Southern Pacific Company granting the latter the right-of-way for laying tracks across a strip of their property at Santa Monica Canyon. Below, Bonifacio Marquez (1838-1891) with his son Miguel (1868-1927).

Pascual Marquez (1844-1916), youngest son of Francisco Marquez, standing left, with Charles Prudhomme, son of Leon Victor Prudhomme. Seated, Don Ause, friend and resident at the Marquez rancho.

Ernest Marquez Collection

The point of land just west of Santa Monica Canyon, angling down to the sea, was the site chosen by Huntington's engineers as the ideal one from which to extend the Long Wharf. The Southern Pacific had secured the right-of-way all along the base of the cliffs, thus excluding any other railroad from building along that route.

Ocean side of the Southern Pacific's tunnel at
Santa Monica. The tunnel was 331 feet long and
braced every three feet by redwood timbers.
At its other end part of the Ocean Avenue bridge
was redesigned and rebuilt to accommodate the
tunnel entrance. Adjacent steps led to the
North Beach Bath House. Structure in background
is the Arcadia Hotel, built in 1886.

By 1893 the Long Wharf itself was nearing
completion. At the mouth of the Canyon
workmen are preparing to sink a well to
supply fresh water to the wharf and the
locomotives.

Thus, barely a month after the Mendell Board's recommendation of San Pedro, the President of the Southern Pacific, having finalized his plans, proceeded to turn them into reality.

In January 1892 the first contract was let for the ambitious Santa Monica project. It was awarded to the firm of Crawley and Marsh and called for construction and tunneling under Ocean Avenue and Colorado Street in Santa Monica, directly in front of the site of the old Los Angeles & Independence Railroad wharf which Huntington had had torn down some 14 years before. Cart gangs began digging into the earth from each end to meet in the middle, a distance of some 331 feet. Right behind them came crews with heavy timbers to hold up the top and walls of the tunnel. Meanwhile, grading went on along the beach at the foot of the bluff all the way to Santa Monica Canyon, where a large working party had begun cutting away a low mesa just to the south, where the grade widened to 125 feet. Dirt from the excavation was used to make a high embankment across the Canyon, leaving room on the north side for a road and the creek. North of the Canyon a grade of about one-half mile was completed.

Twenty men were employed to construct specially built pile drivers, operated by powerful steam engines. These pile drivers were erected on the beach and used to make the trestle at Santa Monica Canyon, before they were put to work on the approach to the Long Wharf itself. By April 20, 1892 all tracks had been laid and ballasted. (The tracks to the Long Wharf began at the Santa Monica Depot. Before entering the tunnel the tracks merged into one single track and remained that way until they passed under the "99 Steps" which descended to the beach from the foot of Oregon Avenue [now Santa Monica Boulevard], where they became two tracks running side by side, with crossover switches at intervals which enabled a train to shift from one track to the other. As they neared Santa Monica Canyon, the tracks increased to three and then reduced to one as they ran over the trestle at the Canyon's mouth. Once over the trestle, the tracks increased to three again, with a series of switches which enabled a train to go out on the Long Wharf, or to the roundhouse at Potrero Canyon, or onto a track that ran past the roundhouse to Temescal Canyon.)

Robert Weinstein Collection

43

Tracks approaching the wharf just west of Santa Monica Canyon. Structure in the center is the roundhouse and turntable for the locomotives. In later years this area was the scene of frequent landslides which would completely cover the tracks with dirt.

In February 1892, a month after work had commenced at Santa Monica, the Senate Commerce Committee was considering an appropriation of $250,000 for San Pedro. To this body Collis Huntington formally announced his decision to abandon that location. In a telegram to Senator Frye the Southern Pacific stated that the ground at San Pedro was so rocky and unstable it was having difficulty driving piles for a new wharf in the outer harbor area, and that it was giving up and was in process of constructing a new wharf at Santa Monica. The item of $250,000 for San Pedro was thereupon thrown out, a stunning manifestation of Huntington's political influence.

Some members of the Committee, however, then began to question whether a harbor at either location was really necessary. The upshot of the ensuing discussion was a decision to appoint another Board of Engineers to re-evaluate both sites and settle the matter of where the deep-water harbor should be once and for all. This time the Board was made up of five engineering officers of the United States Army, and known as the Craighill Board, after Colonel William P. Craighill who headed it. It did not begin its investigations until well into the summer of 1892.

It should be noted that Huntington at this time was still in the midst of a building program at San Pedro, and had spent a considerable amount of money improving older piers and building new ones. When he abandoned the site he retained all his holdings there, even though his efforts now focused on construction of the Long Wharf.

In April 1892, a month or so after the Senate Committee rejected the $250,000 for San Pedro, there arrived in Santa Monica by private railway car as a guest of the Southern Pacific one Adolphus Bonzano, a representative of the Phoenix Bridge Company of Pittsburgh. He had come to inspect Huntington's new adventure. This firm had supplied

The "99 Steps" leading down to the beach from Oregon Avenue (now Santa Monica Boulevard) were raised and rebuilt so that the trains could pass beneath.

45

The Southern Pacific's Long Wharf under construction, with two steam-driven pile drivers at work side by side. The piles, over 90 feet long, of heavily creosoted Oregon pine were driven some 20 feet into the floor of the ocean.

The Long Wharf in 1892, still under construction, with piles of lumber for building the coal bunker and buildings at its "business end" placed along the approach. When the enormous job was finished, 5,084 piles, approximately four million feet of lumber, and innumerable tons of iron bolts and nails had been used.

the railroad magnate with many bridges for his company, and would now be the source of much of the material for the mammoth Long Wharf. For two months after his visit, however, work was at a standstill and the rumor spread that Huntington had abandoned the enterprise because of obstructions in the way of the piles.

It was during this period in the spring and summer of 1892 that a bitter and long-lasting rivalry developed between Redondo and Santa Monica. Redondo saw in a harbor at Santa Monica a threat to its own commercial interests, and took advantage of every opportunity to ridicule and belittle the project, to which taunting the *Santa Monica Evening Outlook* responded with long and scathing articles.

At the time Huntington had informed the Senate Committee of his Santa Monica construction plans the news caused little concern on the part of the San Pedro advocates. Many people thought he had a right to move where he chose, and did not juxtapose his going so with the thought that as a result of

it Santa Monica might supersede San Pedro as the government's choice for a deep-water harbor. The Craighill Board gave public notice that it would be in Los Angeles in July 1892 and that its members would expect all interested persons to be present and to offer such facts as they deemed pertinent to the harbor matter.

The Board's public meetings were held in the rooms of the Los Angeles Chamber of Commerce. Several hundred persons were present, their number about equally divided as to supporters of each of three ports: San Pedro, Redondo, and Santa Monica. Serious consideration of Redondo as a deep-water harbor site was dismissed, because the terrain of the ocean floor there rendered construction of a breakwater impossible.

Collis P. Huntington's representatives formally pressed for the harbor to be located at Santa Monica, and much of the subsequent discussion centered on the ownership of the land in the immediate area of his project, as well as of the land along the beach from Santa Monica to Santa Monica Canyon. Al-

California State Library

though not openly stated at the time, the feeling was rampant that Huntington was creating a monopoly for the Southern Pacific. The hearings were duly concluded, and the results of the Board's deliberations were not made public until the following October.

At about the same time the Craighill Board had arrived in Los Angeles work had resumed at the Santa Monica location. On July 16, 1892 the Southern Pacific announced that a contract to build the "approach" to the Long Wharf had been awarded to the Thomson Wharf Company of San Francisco, and that the Southern Pacific's Chief Engineer, George W. Boschke, would be directing the work. The approach was to be 3,120 feet long and to extend out into the ocean to the five fathom line, some five-eighths of a mile from shore.

Upon completion of the approach, the "business end" of the Long Wharf would be constructed to extend for 1,600 feet beyond the five fathom line, making the entire structure some 4,720 feet long. From the shore the water deepened gradually to 36 feet (six fathoms) at the 3,000-foot line, and varied in depth from 36 to 50 feet along what would

be this last 1,600 feet of wharf, the deck of which was to stand 20 feet above the water line. Thus the largest ships afloat in those years could be easily accommodated.

The length of the business end was determined by the size of the coal bunker that was to be erected there. The Southern Pacific's engineers wanted such a bunker to be long enough to accommodate two colliers at a time, with enough room shoreward for one more ship.

It was also stated that once a breakwater was constructed the area all along the inner harbor would be filled out to a suitable depth with material taken from the hills. The land thus brought into being would be used for mills, lumberyards, etc., and small slips would be built for the use of lumber vessels.

As material for the wharf accumulated, it was stored in long rows on the ground east of Santa Monica proper. Every afternoon four carloads of

Hundreds of carloads of granite rock were dumped along the bank between the wharf and Santa Monica Canyon to protect the roadway and tracks from the high tides. Even so, the tide was high enough in 1915 to wash both road and tracks away.

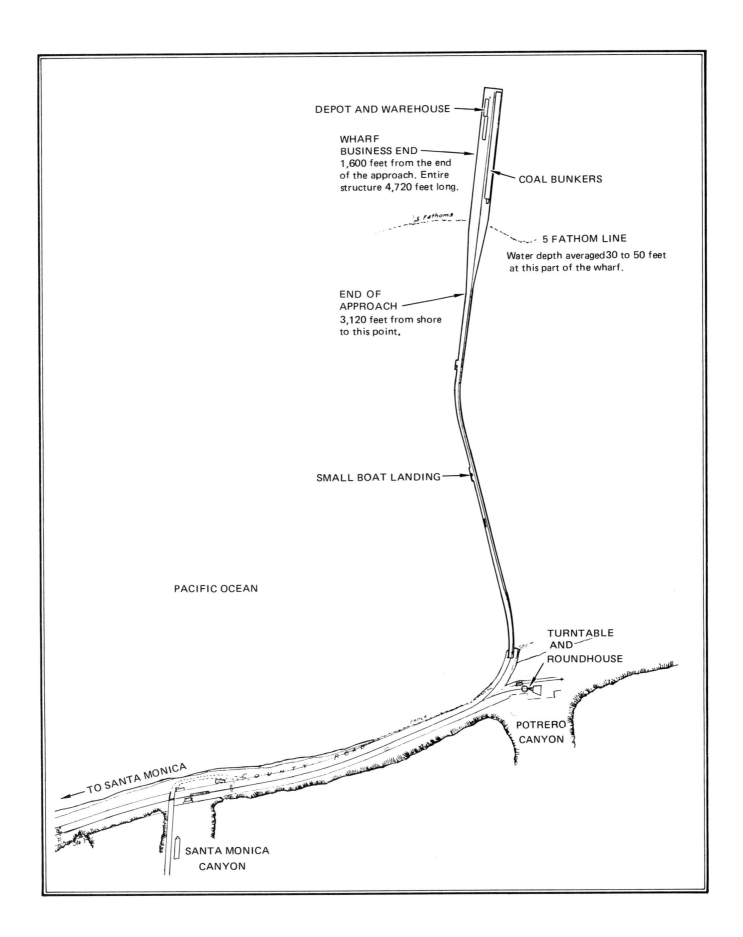

DEPOT AND WAREHOUSE

WHARF
BUSINESS END
1,600 feet from the end
of the approach. Entire
structure 4,720 feet long.

COAL BUNKERS

5 fathoms

5 FATHOM LINE
Water depth averaged 30 to 50 feet
at this part of the wharf.

END OF
APPROACH
3,120 feet from shore
to this point.

SMALL BOAT LANDING

PACIFIC OCEAN

TURNTABLE
AND
ROUNDHOUSE

POTRERO
CANYON

COUNTY ROAD

TO SANTA MONICA

SANTA MONICA
CANYON

50

heavily creosoted piles of Oregon pine would arrive from San Pedro, until the entire supply of 1,500 or more stored there had been transferred to the new location. The idea was to have all the material necessary for the job on hand at the start, to insure its completion without work stoppage. Items were then loaded on cars as needed, and carried the short distance to the construction site at Santa Monica Canyon.

The exact position of the outer end of the Long Wharf was crucial in view of the absence of a breakwater at the time of its construction. Hence engineers spent many days on top of the cliff overlooking the site, observing from morning to night the direction of the swells as they came around Point Dume. They concluded that for the most part their direction was 42°41′E or 42°24′W. So the Long Wharf was to be pointed into the prevailing swells, and to lie nearly southwest and northeast. (Its outer end fell in Latitude 34°1′2″N and Longitude 117° 32′20″W.) Ships tied up at it would also be pointed into the incoming swells, to eliminate their rolling back and forth against the structure.

The approach to the wharf began on the land, just below the cliffs, and ran along the beach, from where it curved to the left out into the ocean, went straight for a distance, and then curved to the right. According to the engineers, the curving provided minimal distance to the five fathom line that would insure a large amount of deep water to westward, and the run along the beach made possible the installation of two 2,000-foot wide side tracks which they felt necessary for handling traffic close to the wharf. Were the approach to have been carried straight out to the water, no more than 800 feet of side track area would have been available.

The roundhouse for the Southern Pacific's locomotives was located at the mouth of Potrero Canyon. Visible at lower right is part of the turntable used to turn the big locomotives. The walkway, 10 feet wide, on the right of the wharf was for pedestrians.

On July 26, 1892 the specially built pile drivers were put into position on the beach and the job of driving the first piles of the Long Wharf into the earth began. The ground at the starting point was extremely hard and the work at first went slowly; but once into the water, progress was rapid. Five kinds of strata were found along the entire length of the wharf: loose cobble, clay, coarse gravel, soft sandrock, and stiff mud.

The width of the approach was 28 feet, to accommodate a double railroad track. Its piles were driven into the ocean floor in rows or "bents" 28 feet in span, with eight piles to a bent and 16 feet between bents. Of the eight piles in each bent, six were placed in groups of three, with a wide space between the groups. Next, the two remaining piles were driven diagonally from opposite ends of the bent, so that they crossed each other in the center. Then the piles were fastened to each other with huge iron spikes and bolts. From the twenty-first bent of the approach onward, the floor of the Long Wharf was of solid wood planking and the center of each track of its double-track railway ran immediately above the second pile on each side.

Plans called for filling in the approach piles with rock fill, but the engineers, uncertain as to how much they would need and how far to extend it, did not rush this part of the job. That turned out to be fortunate, because when the trestle had been carried out to about 320 feet it was noted that there was a great deal of wave action below it, and that the coarse sand and pebbles swashing with the waves were already beginning to cut up the piles. To protect them, each pile in the first 23 bents was spiked from the ocean floor up with three-inch thick planks of Oregon pine. Only when it became certain that beyond that point wave action was not a factor to be concerned about, did the creosoted pile construction continue and the filling-in operation begin. At that time, too, the grade from the Long Wharf back to Santa Monica Canyon was faced with rocks, so as to secure the earth bank on which the tracks were laid from any inroads from the tide. Large quantities of stone were also deposited at the mouth of Santa Monica Canyon, to shield the earth banks there against freshets of water from landward.

51

By September of 1892 the Long Wharf stood at least 1,000 feet out in the ocean, and crowds of people were coming daily to watch the progress of construction. The Craighill Board's report was still pending.

Los Angeles merchants were now beginning to realize that Huntington had undertaken a massive project which would have a major impact on the future commerce of the city, and the latter began to take advantage of this by conducting tours in order to win public support for the installation of a breakwater at Santa Monica. He arranged trips to the Long Wharf on special trains, sending out invitations to visit the site to city officials and prominent businessmen. Those who accepted were treated to a first-class experience.

The special train would run as far as the beginning of the Long Wharf, where the engine would be disconnected and the passenger cars pushed from

In 1892 the Southern Pacific invited city officials and merchants to visit the Long Wharf, then under construction. They were treated to a "grand tour" on trains made up especially for the purpose.

Security Pacific National Bank

behind out onto the wharf itself. The sensation of being suspended over water for such a distance was a heady and exciting one for the riders. From the end of the approach the view at every point was magnificent, extending as it did from Point Dume to the hill at Palos Verdes, with Catalina clearly visible in the distance. And the accompanying Southern Pacific spokesman's verbal projections of great activity to come were as vivid as his argument that this, and not San Pedro, was the ideal spot for a big city's harbor was persuasive. The visitors would return to Los Angeles much impressed, an attitude undoubtedly furthered by the practice of the *Santa Monica Outlook,* whose reporters covered the tours, of publishing not only the names, but also the comments of all who came.

Then, on October 27, 1892, the Craighill Board filed its lengthy and comprehensive report and recommendation, and in December 1892 it was pre-

Southern Pacific train headed back toward the tunnel at Santa Monica. The grade from the beach to the top of the bluff made it necessary for the train to increase its speed in order to make it through the tunnel and up to the depot. Because of the lack of signal communicators, an engineer would on occasion emerge from the dark tunnel to the sudden sight of another train stopped at the depot on the same track, with collision the unavoidable result.

Ernest Marquez Collection

53

Port Los Angeles about 1898. Small building on
the right of the tracks, with smokestack, is the
pumphouse, from where fresh well water was pumped
up to two 50,000-gallon tanks located at the top
of the cliff on the west side of the Canyon.
These were the source of the fresh water supply
for the wharf.

sented to Congress and referred to the House Committee on Rivers and Harbors. The report dealt with every facet of the need for a commercial harbor in the Los Angeles area. It evaluated the commercial and naval aspects of the area and discussed its feasibility as the site for a naval base. It described in technical detail the topography of the section and its general meteorological conditions. It specified what should be the exact location for a breakwater at each considered deep-water harbor site. It listed the results of test borings made to determine the exact contents of the ocean floor. It concluded with a point by point comparison of the Santa Monica and San Pedro locations. And its unanimous recommendation was that San Pedro be selected as the site for a deep-water harbor for Los Angeles.

For a brief time, public discussion of the subject of the harbor location, which had been swelling for several months, ground to a halt. Santa Monica said the Board had made a mistake and would someday regret it. Redondo declared it would abide by the decision and join with Los Angeles to present a united front for San Pedro. Collis P. Huntington said nothing, and the building of the Long Wharf continued.

On December 19, 1892 the last of the 1,500 piles used for the approach to the wharf was driven home. Soon after, the announcement was made that the Thomson Wharf Company would proceed at once with construction of the business end. To hasten the job's completion, three more pile drivers were built, so that by the beginning of 1893 five steam-driven drivers, equipped with 3,000-pound hammers, were working in unison. The piles for the outer end of the wharf had to be well over 90 feet long, in order to be driven some 10 to 20 feet into the ocean floor and still extend upward through 50 feet of water and then rise another 20 feet higher to the floor of the wharf.

Work progressed rapidly on the 1,600 feet of the business end. As it extended from the approach, it gradually, over a distance of 300 feet, spread to its full width of 130 feet, and remained that wide for its last 1,300 feet. Because of the weight of the structures it was to bear, this section of the Long Wharf required many more piles than had been used in the approach.

On its north side, to support the immense coal bunker, the bents were eight feet apart, with nine piles to each bent, all thoroughly braced with a total of 300,000 feet of eight inch by eight inch creosoted timbers and 30 tons of galvanized brace rod, running both vertically and horizontally a little above the surface of high water. On its south side, which supported the depot building, the bents were 12 feet apart, with 14 piles to each bent. The end piles in each bent of the business end were driven into the ocean floor on a slant, from the edge inward, making the structure so strong that it could be destroyed only if it were carried away in a mass. At the ends of each bent on either side of the wharf two fender piles were sunk to absorb any shock from a ship's bumping into it while docking or in a heavy sea.

Mooring piles, capped with iron jackets secured to the wood by cement filling, were driven every 48 feet. Mooring buoys, for ships which arrived by night or at times when there was no available docking space, were also situated in proximity to the wharf. The front moorings on the right had two 7,500-pound and one 14,000-pound anchor, while those on the left had one 5,000-pound and one 14,000-pound anchor. Side mooring buoys, or breast buoys, numbered two on each side, each with a 14,000-pound anchor to hold it in place. These mooring assemblies would supposedly hold a big vessel far enough away from the side of the wharf to keep it from hitting the structure if the water was rough, and could also be used for hauling a ship away from the wharf broadside in case of emergency.

At each of the wharf's two outer corners stood a protective cluster of 16 piles, all braced together, with a light tower mounted atop each cluster, red light for the northwest corner and green light for the southwest. Between these clusters hung an immense bell, which was rung regularly in dark or foggy weather by means of an apparatus operated by the movement of the sea.

The south side of the Long Wharf boasted a walkway some 10 feet wide, running the full length of the approach. At a point beyond the breakers, about 1,200 feet from shore, was a stairway to a boathouse equipped with paraphernalia for sailing, fishing, and other water sports, and a 12-foot by

The impressive coal bunker, 800 feet long, 36 feet wide, and 36 feet high, with a capacity of 8,000 tons. It was divided into four compartments and had 51 chutes through which cars upon the tracks beneath could be loaded all at the same time. Five cranes would lift large buckets of coal from the ships. They were rigged so that they dumped automatically, with one man at the controls operating all five simultaneously.

600-foot fishing platform jutted out over the water.

The greater part of the wharf carried two railroad tracks, but nearing its outer end the number of tracks increased to seven, for maximum safety in the handling of freight. Even when every available docking space was occupied by vessels, all clamoring for a quick discharge of their cargoes, the possibility of an accident was almost nil.

Not far from the land end of the wharf, at the entrance to Potrero Canyon (a short distance north of Santa Monica Canyon), a roundhouse with turntable, together with a coal bunker and a water tank 12 feet high and eight feet in diameter, were erected. Several cabins on the beach nearby, equipped with only outdoor toilets, served as housing for the men working on the wharf.

Track was laid northward beyond the roundhouse to an earth deposit near Temescal Canyon which served as a source for ballast. (The Southern Pacific claimed right-of-way for several miles up the coast north of the wharf, and it was conjectured that the mile of track north from the roundhouse would eventually be part of a line to Ventura.) Ships arriving at the Long Wharf carrying coal and lumber required ballast after they were unloaded and could be supplied with it from this pile of earth by means of a gravity railway, and the land made available by the evacuating of the deposit was slated to be used in the future for warehouses. Vessels which had had to pay $300 to $400 for a load of ballast found they could get it at the Long Wharf for $30 to $60, and this served as an added inducement to shipowners to use the new port.

The largest and most impressive structure on the

wharf was the huge coal bunker. It occupied the final 816 feet on the north side, and some 1,100,-000 feet of lumber and 40 tons of iron had been used in its construction. It was 800 feet long, 36 feet wide, and 36 feet high, with a capacity of 8,000 tons. It was divided into four compartments and had 51 chutes through which cars upon the tracks beneath it could be quickly loaded. Five cranes, which moved from one vessel to another by railroad track, would lift buckets of coal from the ships. They were rigged so they would dump

automatically with one man at the engine operating the entire mechanism. At the shoreward end of the bunker was a powerhouse containing an immense boiler.

The need for a water supply to the Long Wharf had been met by sinking a large well in Santa Monica Canyon, where water was close to the surface, and by means of gigantic pumping equipment lifting the water via three-inch pipes into two 50,000-gallon tanks at the top of the bluff on the Canyon's north side. From there by natural pressure it flowed to the wharf, as well as to the roundhouse at Potrero Canyon. Water was carried at 80 pounds pressure along the entire length of the wharf, through a four-inch pipe equipped with fire plugs at frequent intervals.

Unfortunately, although the water supply system functioned efficiently, the quality of the water turned out to be less than optimum for steampower purposes. Engineers trying to alleviate this problem theorized that since the clay stratum in the area was extremely thick, there was probably better water available beneath it and they could drill through to such a new source. Accordingly, two holes were drilled in the bed of Potrero Canyon. The first well

Total frontage of depot buildings on the south side of the Long Wharf was 384 feet. The farthermost structure is the depot, which housed a large neat waiting room, restrooms, and Post Office; on its second floor were offices for the wharf officials and Customs Deputy, and sleeping rooms for employees. The nearest structure enclosed a warehouse area. Its second story contained two kitchens and dining rooms, one for employees, the other for the public, as well as additional employees' sleeping space. The remaining building served as a one-story freight shed. "No Smoking" warnings can be seen on the structures. The sign under the steps, which was posted at various other places on the wharf also, reads "Discharging of firearms is forbidden."

was carried down 400 feet, at which point the boring tools broke. On the second attempt the tools broke again, a little over 500 feet down, and thereafter the project was abandoned.

The south side of the business end of the wharf, opposite the coal bunker, was taken up by a depot building 384 feet long. Its westernmost end was comprised of an open shed, 55 feet in length, which received freight from the rear hatch of large steamers. Adjoining the shed was a section 133 feet long and two stories high, the lower level of which contained the main offices for the Long Wharf, a large neat waiting room, and restrooms. Above it were other offices, as well as sleeping rooms for employees. Beside this stood a warehouse area 68 feet long and also two stories high. Its upstairs section contained an employees' dining room, a public dining room, a kitchen, and several more sleeping rooms. The remainder of the depot building was a one-story freight shed, 128 feet long.

From the start of its construction the wharf, declared to be "the most perfect wooden pier in existence," had no specifically assigned name, and it was variously referred to as the Santa Monica Wharf, the Long Wharf, the Southern Pacific Wharf, the Southern Pacific's "mammoth wharf," and even as Santa Monica Harbor. Then on April 29, 1893 Collis Huntington bestowed upon it the official designation of Port Los Angeles. He explained that in view of the fact that the wharf was actually located some two miles up the coast from Santa Monica proper, the increasing activity around it would soon result in the formation of a whole new town at the Santa Monica Canyon site, and a local Post Office would be needed for its businessmen. A name, he pointed out, was therefore required, and Port Los Angeles was a striking and effective one, since very few people in the East were aware of Los Angeles' proximity to the ocean. In this Huntington was both manifesting his confidence that he would ultimately succeed in diverting a federal appropriation for a deep-water harbor away from San Pedro to his own colossal enterprise and also attempting, by indirectly giving their city identity as a port, to win support for this from the populace of Los Angeles itself. (A Port Los Angeles Post Office was opened on the wharf on January 11, 1897 and remained in operation until April 30, 1908.)

Less than a week after Huntington had announced the wharf's official name, the Secretary of the Treasury declared that Port Los Angeles had become a sub-port of entry to the Customs District of Los Angeles and that a deputy would be stationed there to collect customs. That meant that vessels from foreign countries could land and discharge their cargoes regardless of their nature. It represented the achievement for Port Los Angeles of all the prestige and advantages usually accruing to an important sub-port of entry.

Even before the official completion of the wharf, vessels began calling at Port Los Angeles. The first of these was the collier *San Mateo,* which arrived on May 11, 1893 with a cargo of 4,200 tons of coal and a group of passengers from San Francisco. The *San Mateo* was a British steamer built in England in 1888 for the Pacific Improvement Company (as mentioned earlier, a subsidiary of the Southern Pacific). She possessed very little in the way of accommodations, so these first passengers to debark at Port Los Angeles were probably company officials and their guests. On this occasion the cargo of the *San Mateo* had to be removed and loaded into railroad cars by manual labor, because the coal bunker was not yet completed. Nevertheless, special trains for people eager to witness the event were run out from Los Angeles. As the steamer tied up to the wharf the Santa Monica Band was playing, and an enthusiastic crowd of 1,000 tossed bouquets of flowers onto her grimy deck. Her Captain, Edward Parks, had "the time of his life" dodging them, and that evening he was honored at a banquet held in the Jackson Hotel in Santa Monica.

Thursday, May 11, 1893: The collier *San Mateo,* carrying a load of coal from British Columbia, as well as passengers picked up at San Francisco, was the first ship to dock at the wharf. Crowds from Los Angeles, carried on special trains, came to witness the historic event. On the weekend many more people came to see the Long Wharf and the *San Mateo.* The latter can be seen unloading coal onto the cars by means of booms mounted on her masts while the coal bunker, on the left side of the wharf, is still under construction. It appears that visitors were free to wander anywhere on the wharf, in spite of the operations of moving locomotives and freight and coal cars.

Port Los Angeles, Southern Pacific Co's Wharf, May 13th 93. Waitz Photo.

Santa Monica continued to grow. This panorama,
taken about 1893 from the roof of the Arcadia
Hotel, shows the empty spot on the other side
of the Ocean Avenue bridge where the Santa Monica
Hotel had stood. The entrance to the tunnel is
on the righthand side of the far end of the
bridge, just opposite the flight of steps leading
up from Eckerts Pavilion. The horse-drawn

trolleys ran from Santa Monica to the Soldiers
Home. They had been developed by William D.
Vawter, and were later sold to the Los Angeles
Pacific Railway when, in 1896, that company
extended its rail line from Los Angeles to Santa
Monica. On the right of the photograph are the
train depot and the Jackson Hotel, at which the
banquet in honor of Captain Wicks and the first
ship to land at the Long Wharf was held.

The Southern Pacific's steam train approaching Port Los Angeles. Roundhouse and turntable at the entrance to Potrero Canyon are visible on the left. Walkway for pedestrians is located on the righthand side of the Long Wharf.

Again, on June 1, 1893, the *San Mateo* arrived from Union Mine, British Columbia, this time carrying 4,300 tons of coal for the Southern Pacific. She had made the trip from Port Los Angeles and back in 14 and a half days, and on Sunday, June 4, many of the thousands of people who visited the Long Wharf also went aboard her for a ship's tour.

That month saw other ships as well docking at the new installation. The big steamer *Santa Rosa* of the Pacific Coast Steamship Company called on her way south. The steamer *Santa Cruz* took on a cargo of 4,062 sacks of barley being shipped to San Francisco by J. J. Millus. And the powerful steam tug *Collis* arrived from San Francisco on June 9, 1893 to be permanently stationed at the Long Wharf to assist vessels in docking and leaving.

On July 14, 1893, to cheers and applause from both workers and onlookers, the last spike connecting the rails to the wharf was driven home by Vice-President Stevenson of the Southern Pacific, who happened by chance to be visiting there that day. Thus, only two years after Collis Huntington's announcement that Santa Monica would become the

major West Coast port, the facilities necessary for the achievement of that status were in operation. Final statistics on the enormous construction job list 5,200 piles, approximately 4,000,000 feet of lumber, and innumerable tons of iron bolts and nails.

By October 1893 the depot had been completed, and its public restaurant was the scene of an elaborate banquet held to celebrate the completion of Port Los Angeles and to honor Thomas Thomson and the excellent job done by his Thomson Wharf Company. It was an exciting and dramatic event for all the dignitaries and guests attending. Everyone who had been even remotely involved in the construction of the Long Wharf was commended and congratulated. Toasts were offered continuously and speeches, one after the other, took up every minute of the affair. These speeches were so

The two tracks on the approach to the "business end" of the Long Wharf expanded to seven as the wharf broadened to its full width of 130 feet, remaining that wide for its last 1,300 feet.

numerous and long-winded that many who came prepared to speak were never given a chance to do so. One such person was Lemuel T. Fisher, owner of the *Santa Monica Outlook,* and from the beginning, a loyal and staunch advocate of Santa Monica as the harbor site. He printed his entire speech in his newspaper the next day.

Officials of the port were A. M. Jamison, Agent; T. M. Polhemus, Chief Clerk; F. H. Oswald and W. T. Maher, Clerks; and Captain F. E. Dornfield, General Supervisor of the wharf and in charge of the tug *Collis.*

People from all walks of life and from all over the world now came to view the Long Wharf. Thousands arrived each weekend on special trains set up to handle the crowds. It was an exciting sightseeing attraction, and visitors could walk the entire length of the wharf, spend hours watching sailing ships and steamers coming and going, and enjoy the restaurant. Fishing from the new wharf became a popular activity, and catches of 15-pound yellowtail and halibut were not uncommon.

Whenever a governor or any important official of a State appeared in the Los Angeles area, he would of course be given the grand tour by the Southern Pacific. Thoroughly impressed and awed by the immense structure, the official would be told that he should impress on the Senators from his State, if he had not already done so, the importance of throwing their support to Santa Monica rather than San Pedro as the site for a deep-water harbor for Los Angeles, since as he could clearly see Port Los Angeles was the logical place for one.

Earlier in that year of 1893, just after the Craig-hill Board filed its report, the Los Angeles Chamber of Commerce had sent a representative to Washington to lay the foundation for an appropriation for San Pedro. He went armed with petitions from businessmen from every area of Southern California, and even from Arizona and New Mexico, and with resolutions passed by the Redlands and the

Land approach to the Long Wharf from Santa Monica Canyon

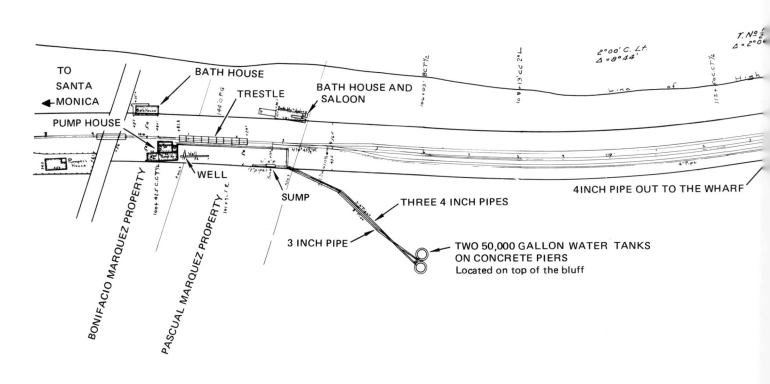

PACIFIC OCEAN

TO SANTA ◄MONICA

BATH HOUSE

TRESTLE

BATH HOUSE AND SALOON

PUMP HOUSE

WELL

SUMP

THREE 4 INCH PIPES

3 INCH PIPE

4 INCH PIPE OUT TO THE WHARF

TWO 50,000 GALLON WATER TANKS
ON CONCRETE PIERS
Located on top of the bluff

BONIFACIO MARQUEZ PROPERTY

PASCUAL MARQUEZ PROPERTY

SANTA MONICA CANYON

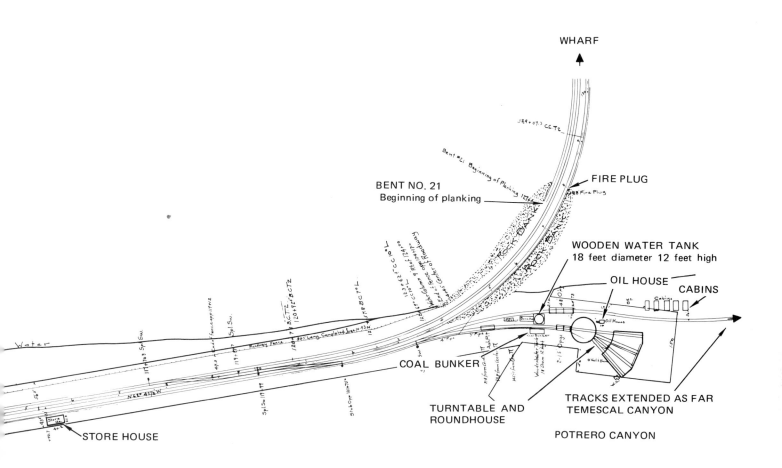

WHARF

BENT NO. 21
Beginning of planking

FIRE PLUG

WOODEN WATER TANK
18 feet diameter 12 feet high

OIL HOUSE   CABINS

COAL BUNKER

TURNTABLE AND
ROUNDHOUSE

TRACKS EXTENDED AS FAR
TEMESCAL CANYON

POTRERO CANYON

STORE HOUSE

Zola Clearwater Collection

The immense size of the coal bunker can be
visualized from this photograph of Port Los
Angeles taken from the Pacific Palisades.

Riverside Town Trustees, the Boards of Trade of Pasadena and of San Pedro, the Supervisors of San Bernardino, and the California State Board of Trade, all stating they were generally in favor of the decision of the Army engineers.

A bill which included an appropriation of $250,-000 for the commencement of work at San Pedro was indeed introduced; but this measure never got out of the Senate Commerce Committee of which Senator Frye, who had commented four years earlier on the seeming appropriateness of Santa Monica Bay as a port site, was still the Chairman. Also a member of the Committee at this time was Senator Jones of Nevada, whose real, if unofficial, home had been in Santa Monica since the construction of his ill-fated Los Angeles & Independence Railroad. Along about this time Senator Jones, invoking the tradition of "senatorial courtesy," asked of Senator Frye that should the matter of an appropriation for a harbor for Los Angeles come up while he, Jones, was absent from the capital, it not be con-

sidered until he had returned to Washington. Predictably, respect for their fellow Senator's request restrained the Committee from taking any action on the matter through the winter of 1893.

Meanwhile, from that year through the next, some 300 vessels arrived at Port Los Angeles, carrying passengers as well as cargoes of coal, lumber, railroad ties, and rails. Los Angeles merchants who now used the port to receive and ship goods highly commended the mammoth wharf for its modern and efficient facilities. The Pacific Coast Steamship Company announced that its large ships would no longer stop at San Pedro, but only at Port Los Angeles, and a considerable amount of business that had formerly moved in and out of San Pedro and Redondo was now moving through the new installation.

Early in 1894 Collis Huntington came to Santa Monica to inspect his new venture, and voiced his enthusiasm and pleasure at its progress and potential. Then he dropped in unannounced at the offices of the Los Angeles Chamber of Commerce and asked for a conference with its officers on the subject of "local harbor improvements." Those few Chamber officials who could be rounded up on such

View from the roof of the roundhouse. Coal smoke is billowing from a locomotive pulling passenger cars back to Los Angeles.

67

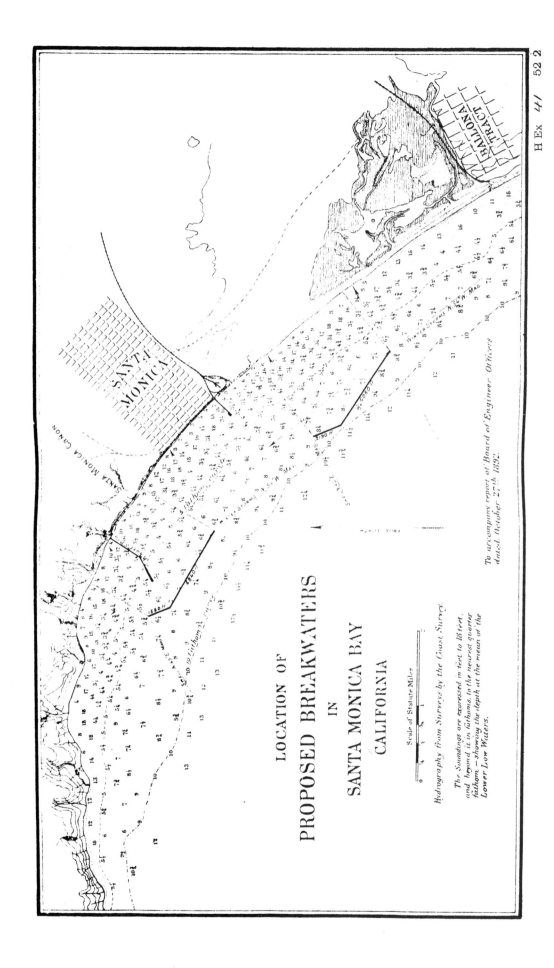

LOCATION OF

PROPOSED BREAKWATERS

IN

SANTA MONICA BAY

CALIFORNIA

Scale of Statute Miles

Hydrography from Surveys by the Coast Survey.

The Soundings are expressed in feet to 18 feet,
and beyond it in fathoms, to the nearest quarter
fathom.—showing the depth at the mean of the
Lower Low Waters.

To accompany report of Board of Engineer Officers
dated October 27th 1892.

short notice were fully aware of his commitment to a breakwater at Santa Monica, as opposed to their organization's stand for San Pedro, and were somewhat reticent about discussing the harbor issue with him on their own and in such an informal meeting, as a result of which, perhaps, the railroad magnate found himself doing most of the talking. His approach was somewhat less than diplomatic: "You people are making a big mistake in supporting this San Pedro appropriation . . . I do not find it to my advantage to have this harbor built at San Pedro, and I shall be compelled to oppose all efforts that you . . . make to secure appropriations for that site . . ." He spoke openly of having "some little influence at Washington" and, working up a bit of a lather in the face of his hearers' failure to react, wound up by banging the table and declaring: "Well, I don't know, for sure, that I can get this money for Santa Monica; I think I can. But I know damned well that you shall never get a cent for that other place."

Contrary to most such scenarios, however, Huntington did not then stomp angrily out of the room, but instead assumed a smiling and gracious attitude and invited the Chamber's Board of Directors to go down to Santa Monica the next day to inspect Port Los Angeles for themselves. His invitation was accepted, and about a dozen Los Angeles Chamber of Commerce board members made up the party on Huntington's private train. They visited the wharf and then retired to the Arcadia Hotel for "refreshments." Just how much impact this particular sequence of events had on the pro-San Pedro policy of the Chamber of Commerce is not known, but in ensuing months it became evident that the attitude of the Chamber's membership toward the harbor issue was nowhere near as unanimous as had been assumed.

Thus, in spite of the "once and for all" settlement of the question by the Craighill Board, argument continued over where the deep-water harbor should be located, i.e., where a breakwater should be installed. Local Santa Monica boosters were strong in number and to them could be added many influential members of the House and Senate who were "friends" of Huntington and could be depended upon to vote for Port Los Angeles regardless of *any* arguments offered in favor of San Pedro.

The battle heated up again, and the local newspapers took their stands. The *Los Angeles Herald* (soon to be sold and under new ownership change its position in the matter), the *Los Angeles Express,* and the *Santa Monica Outlook* went with Huntington and Port Los Angeles. The *Los Angeles Times* supported San Pedro. Actually the *Los Angeles Times* had published its first editorial on the subject almost a year before, in the spring of 1893, which said in part:

> The recent Board of Engineers have settled upon San Pedro as the location for the harbor, confirming the judgment of the former Board. We have thus a unanimous decision from eight distinguished authorities, based on technical grounds, in favor of that site. It is the invariable custom of Congress to grant appropriations in accordance with the findings of its own engineers. It is therefore idle to discuss the question of the possibility of securing help for another site than San Pedro. The Southern Pacific people are disposed to favor Port Los Angeles, where they are constructing a wharf. Their enterprise in developing commerce through a new port is commendable and will elicit such patronage as it merits; but that is not the real point at issue. The influence of the Southern Pacific at Washington may be great — perhaps greater than it should be — but it cannot reach to the extent of upsetting all the established precedents that govern harbor appropriations, and even if it were so powerful, it would still be the plain duty of the people of this section and their representatives to oppose a scheme to use government funds against the advice of its technical authorities, for the special use and benefit of a single corporation.

In March 1894, not long after Huntington's visit, the Chamber of Commerce met to adopt some resolutions on the harbor site and to consider the advisability of again sending a special delegate to Washington to represent the commercial interests of Los Angeles. This session turned into a long and lively debate, which was then prolonged from meeting to meeting by one parliamentary procedure or another. At the outset it appeared that a majority of the members would be for San Pedro, but as argument continued Santa Monica supporters gained strength. On more than one occasion an adjournment was secured just when the matter was about to be brought to a vote. Finally the date of April

7, 1894 was set for a decision on whether the Chamber would adopt Santa Monica or San Pedro as its choice for the breakwater installation. Chamber membership at that time was about 550 persons. Of the 464 ballots cast, five were "scattered," and the others divided into 328 for San Pedro and 131 for Santa Monica.

This vote of the Los Angeles Chamber was regarded as another "final" settlement of the matter, and since all of its members were leading merchants of Los Angeles the decision did do much to strengthen the cause of San Pedro. A number of Santa Monica supporters now decided to go along with the majority and became enthusiastic workers on the anti-Southern Pacific side. Had the vote gone the other way it surely would have shattered the Chamber's standing with the people, but it would have supplied Santa Monica with the one thing it did not have, an official and authoritative public expression in favor of Port Los Angeles.

A few months later, in June 1894, the Senate Commerce Committee was again considering the San Pedro-Santa Monica question. The Los Angeles representatives stated their case for San Pedro, but they were followed by Collis Huntington himself, who asked the Committee for a $4,000,000 appropriation for a breakwater at Santa Monica.

At the same Committee meeting E. L. Corthell, an engineer employed by the Southern Pacific, delivered a lengthy presentation of the advantages of the Santa Monica site and discussed his proposal for a breakwater there. Corthell explained that rock for the breakwater was obtainable from three sources, two of them on the lines of the Southern Pacific and the third at Catalina Island. He declared it would not be feasible to rely on Catalina for any huge quantities of stone, since its docking facilities were limited and there was room for only two barges. It would also be risky to count on hauling rock from there during the winter months when the sea was heavy. The mainland sources, however, were another matter. One of the two land quarries was located near the end of the Southern Pacific's tracks at Chatsworth in the San Fernando Valley, a point whence it was downgrade all the way to Port Los Angeles. It offered an unlimited supply of sandstone. Five trains a day, made up of 30 cars each of which would carry 20 tons of rock, could

easily be dispatched from there and their contents dumped into the ocean at Port Los Angeles. The other quarry was at Declez, adjacent to Colton and near the main line of the Southern Pacific 60 miles east of Los Angeles. The stone there was pure granite, suitable for any area of the breakwater. It was estimated that there were about six billion cubic yards of rock available, all under Southern Pacific control. Five daily trains of 20-ton cars could also be hauled from this location, for a total output from it and the Chatsworth source of about 6,000 tons of rock daily.

Corthell went on to point out that the Long Wharf itself could be utilized for more efficient construction of a breakwater, that it would be a simple matter to extend a trestle from the end of the wharf to the breakwater location, curving the trestle to conform to the shape of the sea wall, so that both ends of the latter could be under construction simultaneously.

Now, for the first time, the attention of the newspapers of other States began to be attracted to the California harbor matter. Several New York, Chicago, and St. Louis papers published articles on the subject. The *New York World* of June 26, 1894 was particularly hard on Senator Jones:

> The advantages which the building of an artificial harbor at Santa Monica would bring to Senator Jones personally, it is difficult to overestimate. The official record sheds some light on the subject. The County records of Los Angeles show that the property adjoining the exclusive waterfront of the Southern Pacific is divided into eight holdings. The title to parcels one, two and eight are in the names of John P. Jones and Arcadia B. de Baker. They constitute three-quarters of all the lands situated as described. All the remainder of the land with the exception of a few feet at the mouth of Santa Monica Canyon is in the name of Frank H. Davis, representing Mr. Huntington. It will be seen that Mr. Huntington's Santa Monica enterprise throughout its entire extent is as exclusive as though it were surrounded by a Chinese Wall.

After that Senator Jones became more moderate, although his votes never departed from the Huntington cause.

The *St. Louis Democrat* carried full reports of the proceedings and from those of June 26 to July

The tracks along the beach to the Long Wharf
were the exclusive property of the Southern
Pacific Railroad. Land seen in the above
photograph, along the beach and on top of
the cliffs as far as Santa Monica Canyon,
was owned by two people — Senator John P. Jones
and Arcadia Bandini de Baker.

9, 1894 the following paragraphs are culled:

 . . . The harbor contest at Los Angeles waxes warmer. C. P. Huntington was seen going the rounds of the hotels today, and although it was Sunday, he made no halt in buttonholing Senators. Four days ago there was a decided majority in the Commerce Committee in favor of following the wishes of the two Senators from California, but since the arrival of Mr. Huntington at the capital it is now a matter of great doubt where the majority will be found. There is serious speculation in the minds of many people as to the means Mr. Huntington may have used to bring about this change.

 . . . For three hours the battle of San Pedro against Santa Monica for government recognition as the Los Angeles Harbor waged today in the room of the Senate Committee on Commerce. Huntington, the Southern Pacific magnate, paced the corridors, and asked anxiously after news, whenever anyone came out of the committee room, and betrayed a degree of nervousness wholly unusual to him. Ordinarily Mr. Huntington is philosophical and composed. Today he was "rattled" as no one remembers to have seen him, in his many visits to the capital.

 . . . One of a series of telegrams, from J. W. Reinhart, president of the Santa Fe, to Mr. R. C. Karens, shows how much is at stake in this contest: "Atchison is too much interested with its $500,000,000 of property, to permit it to be held out of Pacific Ocean business by the Southern Pacific, whose prayer, if granted, would shut out Atchison and create absolute monopoly. Atchison is the only railway line, other than the Southern Pacific, reaching Southern California. If the appropriation goes to Huntington, it throttles all chances of competition, besides permanently injuring the growth of California and adjacent States and territories.

Such attention from the press in diverse parts of the country was not the only factor in promoting what was in a sense a local controversy into a matter of national interest. For in the winter of 1894, in an admirable example of capitalizing on circumstances, E. A. Forrester of the Board of Supervisors, noting the emigrant nature of the rapidly-growing population of Los Angeles, suggested that numerous members of that city's Chamber of Commerce might be acquainted with members of Congress from other States. A list of United States legislators was sent to every Chamber member, with a request that he indicate those names on it with which he might be familiar from years of residence elsewhere. The results were striking, in that 200 of the Chamber's members responded and, overall, named officials from almost every State in the Union. Such members then readily sent to those Congressmen and Senators, along with a personal note, a strongly-worded circular letter urging them to take a stand against commercial monopoly in Los Angeles. How the sting of such a series of small stones from the public's slingshot compared with the solid clout of the Southern Pacific cannot, of course, be assessed. But on the basis of the number of responses received by the senders, it is safe to say that, in those less sophisticated and less media-saturated times, the project was both imaginative and worthwhile.

Collis Huntington's chief supporters on the Senate Commerce Committee in that summer of 1894 were Senators Frye of Maine, Jones of Nevada, Dolph of Oregon, and the new Chairman, Senator Ransom of North Carolina, who had unexpectedly switched from a San Pedro advocate to a warm supporter of Santa Monica. These men were prepared to give Huntington the $4,000,000 he had asked for. Senators Cullom of Illinois, Berry of Arkansas, and White of California were for San Pedro. The other members of the Committee were either wavering or absent. Encouraged by this cloudy situation, Senator Frye moved successfully to defer a decision until the following year so that Committee members could visit Santa Monica and San Pedro to study at first hand the merits of both sites. This was obviously a play for time on his part, because no provision was made for expenses and no definite date set for them to go.

By 1895 the Los Angeles Chamber of Commerce had grown so big and was concerned with such varied interests that it could no longer devote time to any active fight for a deep-water harbor at San Pedro. As a result, a new group was formed whose sole purpose was to secure an appropriation for a breakwater there. This organization was called the Free Harbor League, and it enlisted some 400 members. The implication in its name was obvious,

Senator William B. Frye of Maine was Chairman of the Senate Committee on Commerce during most of the period of the "harbor issue." He was a determined and unwavering foe of San Pedro, and his position made it possible for him to block, year after year, any appropriations for that site. He did so openly and without hesitation, and as a "friend" of Collis Huntington consistently led the pro-Santa Monica contingent in Congress.

i.e., that an official harbor for Los Angeles at Santa Monica would represent a monopoly, while one at San Pedro would be a free harbor, open to any merchant or railroad who wanted to use it.

No further action occurred at the time, however. The long delay on the part of Congress had dampened public enthusiasm and many people were simply tired of the issue. At a meeting of the Free Harbor League a member suggested that possibly Huntington, too, was tired of it and another member, who was friendly with the latter's local representatives, was given the job of checking this out. He reported back that Huntington had indeed become exasperated with the situation and had agreed to a truce, and that for the duration of that session of Congress he would make no move. The League relaxed and accepted this, and in view of the depleted state of the national treasury submitted to the House of Representatives' Committee on Rivers and Harbors a request for a mere $392,000 to further improve San Pedro's inner harbor, a move supported by both Senators from California, as well as by all the State's Congressmen.

In connection with this request for $392,000 the League elected four of its most active members to constitute a special delegation to go to Washington and lay it before the House Committee, which set the date of February 17, 1896 for its presentation. . No sooner had the delegates been heard, and their

Buttons worn by the San Pedro and "Free Harbor" boosters.

S.P. MAMMOTH WHARF, 4700 FT.
19.   PORT LOS ANGELES, CAL.

The "business end" of the Long Wharf, with ships
unloading their cargoes of lumber and coal. A
huge loading boom can be seen on the center mast
of the sailing ship on the right. Tied to the
sides of the ship are pilings, to be dropped
into the ocean, towed to shore, and there loaded
onto cars. The tall smokestack in front of the
coal bunker marks the powerhouse, where a giant
steam boiler generated the steampower to
operate the coal-loading booms.

View of the deck of a three-masted ship tied
up to the south side of Port Los Angeles,
probably about 1905.

77

Late 1890's: View looking toward Port Los Angeles from the roof of the Arcadia Hotel.

proposition duly "taken under advisement" by the House Rivers and Harbors Committee, when Collis Huntington appeared in person before a meeting of the Senate Commerce Committee and presented that body with a request for $3,098,000 for a breakwater at Port Los Angeles.

The Free Harbor League's reaction to Huntington's move was one of worry and bewilderment, for it had been assured by its sympathizers on the Washington scene that no major appropriation could possibly be made that year, because the party in power was absolutely determined to cut expenditures to the bone. Indeed, it was on the basis of these assurances that the League had elected to ask only for an appropriation for development of the inner harbor and not to broach the question of a San Pedro breakwater at that time. It should be noted perhaps that this decision was not an entirely self-sacrificing one. The League's theory was that every dollar committed to San Pedro for any purpose would attach the government more securely to the concept of that location as the official port for the city of Los Angeles.

The mystery was at least partially illuminated the following month, when Congressman Binger Hermann of Oregon, Chairman of the Sub-Committee on the Pacific Coast of the Rivers and Harbors Committee, revealed in a letter to one of the members of the Free Harbor League's delegation that he was in favor of a bill that would appropriate funds for *both* San Pedro and Santa Monica. "Your county," he wrote "should have both great works . . . and later on . . . a project for a still deeper draft should be insisted on for San Pedro." To make matters worse for the Free Harbor League's cause, Congressman Hermann went on to say "if one goes the other must take the same course." In other words, if Huntington's request were to be ignored so would be San Pedro's.

With this the Free Harbor League collapsed into a state of consternation and incredulity. Its members may not have been immune to the boosterism of that period, but they were American taxpayers, too, and could not see themselves privy to the colossal expenditures that would be involved in developing two separate deep-water harbors for their city

Looking south toward Southern Pacific tunnel. In background, the Arcadia Hotel. To right, the North Beach Bath House and stub of the Los Angeles & Independence wharf.

Ernest Marquez Collection

79

About 1890: Deadman's Island stands at the
entrance to San Pedro Harbor. In the foreground
are stacks of railroad ties, lumber, and piles.

when only one would more than suffice. One of the
League's representatives in Washington made immediate inquiries of the Chairman of the Committee
on Rivers and Harbors and was assured by him
that such a double appropriation was a rumor with
no basis in fact.

In spite of such reassurance, the report of the
Committee as prepared for submission to the House
of Representatives, an advance copy of which was
secured by a *San Francisco Examiner* reporter and
telegraphed to Los Angeles, did indeed recommend
both an appropriation of $392,000 for San Pedro
and one of $3,098,000 for Port Los Angeles. Ad-
vocates of the former went into an uproar. Congressman McLachlan, who represented the Los
Angeles area but was not himself a member of the
Rivers and Harbors Committee, woke up to a night-
mare of thousands of telegrams and letters from

outraged constituents. In turn, he dutifully descended upon Congressman Hermann only to be
told: "The people of your District are a set of idiots
that don't know when they are well off, if they can't
take a double appropriation and two harbors, when
they have only asked for one . . . Allright, both
those items go out of the bill now, do you hear? If
you won't take Santa Monica, you don't get San
Pedro." And at a meeting of the Rivers and Harbors Committee that same day he moved that, in
view of telegrams he had received from Los Angeles citizens in general and from the Free Harbor
League in particular protesting the appropriation
for Santa Monica, and in view of the fact that the
Congressman from the District was also opposed to
it, *all* sums set aside for the County of Los Angeles
be stricken from the bill. In spite of what might appear to be an absence of logic in this resolution, the
motion was carried. (Subsequently, an appropriation for $50,000 for a dredging of the inner harbor
of San Pedro, for reasons unknown to this writer

Looking towards Terminal Island in 1897.

introduced by a Committee Congressman from Minnesota, was inserted and appeared in the bill when it was formally presented to the House of Representatives on April 6, 1896.)

Suddenly the "harbor issue" had become not a question of San Pedro versus Santa Monica, but of a deep-water harbor at Santa Monica and improvements at San Pedro, or nothing at all for either site. Thus did the Free Harbor League's strategy of going along with the policy of reducing federal expenses while at the same time cutting the government's options as to a final choice run jarringly aground. From the debacle three factions now emerged: pro San Pedro and against anything for Santa Monica; pro Santa Monica and against anything for San Pedro, except possibly just enough to complete development of its inner harbor; and pro double appropriation.

The average citizen of Los Angeles at this time was in favor of San Pedro, primarily because on two different occasions government engineers had declared it to be a more preferable location for a deep-water harbor than Santa Monica. To this intelligent enough conclusion, he added his acceptance of the charge that in Port Los Angeles Huntington had laid the groundwork for an impressively profitable monopoly for himself and his Southern Pacific. When he read or heard that the House of Representatives might be going to vote on a Rivers and Harbors Bill which contained appropriations for both places, he at first refused to believe it. To assume that the federal government would even consider taking on the cost of two deep-water harbors within 20 miles of each other, along a coastline otherwise devoid of any such harbor for a distance of 600 miles, struck him as preposterous.

Meanwhile, the bill in question, now stripped of significant appropriations for either place, was passed by the House of Representatives and forwarded to the Senate Commerce Committee. On April 16, 1896 that body began its hearings on the matter. Free Harbor League representatives laid before its members their arguments in favor of San Pedro, as did Senator White of California, himself a Committee member. Their importunings were futile, because the majority on the Committee was not to be swayed. There also appeared before the Committee at this time a pro-Santa Monica delegation, which preferred to be known as the "double harbor delegation," one of whose members was a Director of the Los Angeles Chamber of Commerce. This group was openly sympathetic to Collis Huntington, claimed that he was the victim of prejudiced attacks, and insisted that the people of Los Angeles really didn't care where a deep-water harbor was located, as long as it was someplace near their city.

Under the gavel of Senator Frye, once again its Chairman, the Senate Commerce Committee voted 9 to 6 to restore the $3,098,000 Santa Monica appropriation to the bill, and on May 8, 1896 its version reached the floor of the Senate. From *The Free Harbor Contest at Los Angeles,* by Charles D. Willard, comes the following:

> When the bill emerged from the committee, it carried a majority and a minority report. . . . The majority report on the Santa Monica item was a brief document, containing about 150 words. It would seem that a proposition so extraordinary — the appropriation of so large a sum at such a time for a locality that had been ruled against by the engineering authorities of the government, and which was opposed by all the representatives from the State, both the Senators and by nearly all the people of the adjacent district — called for a good deal of explaining. But the majority had very little to say. The count of the votes in the committee and Mr. Huntington's lobby assured them that a majority of the Senate could be relied upon.

Among the signers of the minority report on the Rivers and Harbors Bill was Senator Stephen M. White, native son of California, born in San Francisco in 1853. White's parents were natives of Ireland. His father, William F. White, grew up in Pennsylvania and with his wife, Fannie Russell White, arrived in San Francisco in 1849. The future United States Senator was educated in that city and received his college degree at the age of 18.

In 1874 he was admitted to the State Bar and shortly afterward moved to Los Angeles, where in 1883 he became District Attorney. In 1886 White was elected to the State Senate and the following year, upon the death of the Governor and the accession of the Lieutenant Governor to his office, he became Acting Lieutenant Governor of California.

By 1892, the year the Democrats succeeded in electing Grover Cleveland to the presidency, White had become a prominent figure in the national councils of the Democratic Party, and the California State Legislature elected him to the United States Senate for the six-year term beginning in March 1893. Almost immediately he was given an appointment to the Senate Commerce Committee, and it was assumed that as a Californian, and coming from Los Angeles at that, he would involve himself rapidly and deeply in the harbor issue.

Contrary to expectations, through the first few years of his term the new Senator merely "did his duty" by the harbor question. When delegates from Los Angeles organizations came to the nation's capital, he would indeed arrange for them to present their views before the Committee but he did little more than that.

Actually, Senator White, well aware of the tremendous power of the Huntington lobby, was quite simply waiting for the proper moment to launch a major attack. When the 1896 Rivers and Harbors Bill came before the full Senate, he deemed that moment to have arrived. The arguments on the Senate floor over the form in which it should be passed went on for five days. The leading opponent of its contents was Stephen M. White, and when the struggle was over he emerged from it a political hero and Los Angeles' shining knight.

Senator Stephen M. White who, after his victory over Collis P. Huntington and the Southern Pacific interests, emerged as Los Angeles' hero.

83

Senator White proposed an amendment to the Rivers and Harbors Bill which would strike the $3,098,000 for Santa Monica, and provide instead that an appropriation of that same amount go to *either* Santa Monica *or* San Pedro, with the decision to be made by still another special Board of Engineers, whose members should consist of (1) an officer of the United States Navy with a rank no lower than Commander, to be appointed by the Secretary of the Navy; (2) a member of the Army Corps of Engineers, to be appointed by the Secretary of War; and (3) a member of the Coast Geodetic Survey, to be appointed by the Superintendent of the Coast Geodetic Survey.

Even more to the real point of the issue, however, was the stipulation in the White Amendment that should the decision go in favor of Santa Monica, the Southern Pacific would agree to allow any other railroad to use the tracks and wharf at Port Los Angeles and pay a proportionate part of the cost.

In support of his amendment Senator White then presented to the Senate a thorough recapitulation of the entire harbor fight from its very beginning. He displayed maps and photographs of the two harbors, and delivered an exhaustive description of their physical features. He offered testimony from over 40 different shipmasters as to the holding ground and benefits of San Pedro. He discussed at length the monopoly feature of the Santa Monica site, and described the difficulty other railroads would encounter seeking entry to that harbor. His presentation took up two entire days of Senate session. Senator Frye then consumed another day's session with his arguments for Santa Monica, consulting frequently with Huntington in the process, and Huntington himself talked to White in an unsuccessful effort to win him over. At last, after almost a week of debate and compromise, the White Amendment was passed.

In its final form it called for the appointment of a Board of five engineers, one from the Navy, one from the Coast and Geodetic Survey, and three from civil life, to be named by the President of the United States. The $392,000 for improvements to San Pedro's inner harbor was restored. The amended bill now passed both the Senate and the House, only to be vetoed by President Cleveland, on the grounds that the Treasury was not prepared to meet such enormous expenditures. The President's veto was overridden, and the Act became law in June 1896.

This was not the only time the Southern Pacific lost out to the people in those years. In addition to the lobbyists and elected officials working for Huntington to assure that Port Los Angeles would become the official harbor for Los Angeles, there were also some 28 paid lobbyists and attorneys employed at the nation's capital on an entirely different matter of truly nationwide concern in which he was involved, an attempt by the Southern Pacific to influence Congress to pass the Pacific Railroad Refunding Bill. This was a bill, prepared by Huntington, which would wipe out a debt of more than $60,000,000 owed to the government by the Southern Pacific. It was no secret that the company intended to default on this debt. The bill in part provided for the refunding of the debt into bonds bearing two per cent interest and payable at a period estimated at 80 years from date, a time so far in the future as to be unrealistic and to indicate that the debt never would be paid. It was well known in Washington that this piece of legislation was to be rammed through Congress by the Republican machine, to which Huntington had always contributed generously, and had it not been for William Randolph Hearst and Ambrose Bierce, the plan might well have succeeded.

One of the most intensive and longest-lived crusades ever carried out by Hearst's *San Francisco Examiner* was its battle against Collis Huntington. Shortly after taking over as editor of the *Examiner,* Hearst had hired Ambrose Bierce as a columnist and given this eccentric author, whose pen was perhaps the most caustic and vitriolic of all American writers of the period, almost carte blanche as to commentary on the American scene. Bierce was a Southern Pacific enemy of long standing, and he now went to Washington and at the rate of an article a day sarcastically exposed the dishonesty built into the railroad's bill and the real reasons why the Republican machine was committed to its passage. His steady ridicule proved a powerful and effective influence, and the Railroad Refunding Act was defeated in the House of Representatives by a vote of 168-102.

Santa Monica Canyon was not destined to develop
into the new town of Port Los Angeles which
Huntington had envisioned. By 1896 it was still
the site of no more than a few stores and a dance
pavilion. The barns in the photograph belonged
to Miguel Marquez.

Rear Admiral John C. Walker headed the Engineering Board that made the final decision that San Pedro, not Santa Monica, was the logical site for the deep-water harbor.

The appointments to the new Board of Engineers were made the following October. It was headed by Rear Admiral Walker. Prior to holding public hearings the Walker Board spent weeks studying the technical aspects of the question, with the help of charts, maps, and other data from the Coast Geodetic Survey. Then it devoted two months to a complete and practical on-site investigation of each of the two harbor areas. New soundings were taken and fresh charts prepared. Borings were made all along the sites of the proposed breakwaters. A primary characteristic of these efforts was faithful and thorough work, so that the losing side in the dispute could make no claim that the investigation had been in any way a superficial one. The Walker Board's

hearings began at the Los Angeles Chamber of Commerce rooms on December 21, 1896. Although seven days were devoted to them, very little that was new was offered by either the Santa Monica or the San Pedro proponents.

On March 1, 1897, almost 10 years after Los Angeles commercial interests had appealed for government funds to the end that their city might have a deep-water harbor, the Walker Board filed its decision in favor of San Pedro. There was band music and dancing in the streets of Los Angeles in celebration of the event. Happy San Pedro advocates estimated it would take two months for specifications to be drawn up and perhaps another 60 days for advertising and evaluation of bids. Thus work on the harbor should be under way in four months at the most. Their optimism in this regard, however, was to prove unjustified.

For implementation of the harbor project at the federal level now became the responsibility of General Russel A. Alger, the Secretary of War. And as fate would have it, General Alger was an old friend of Collis Huntington, through a business association with the latter in lumber interests in the northwest. In fact, when the harbor battle was at its height he had visited Los Angeles as the guest of the Southern Pacific, and expressed his opinion that Santa Monica was the preferable location, an opinion from which the Walker Board's decision had not caused him to depart.

This gentleman now adopted a series of deliberate delaying tactics, in order to stall the monetary appropriation and, somehow, get the issue before Congress still another time. He responded to complaints about delay from Los Angeles with bland and empty promises that he would proceed with the matter, but that the Walker Board's report was vague and more study would be required first. When, at Senator White's behest, the Senate inquired of General Alger why he was not moving ahead, the latter replied with a letter in which he listed several different reasons for the delay, all of which drew hoots of derision and howls of outrage from Los Angeles, where it was now realized that the Secretary of War was a Huntington puppet and that another battle was on.

The Senate reacted to Alger's letter with a resolution instructing him to advertise for bids immedi-

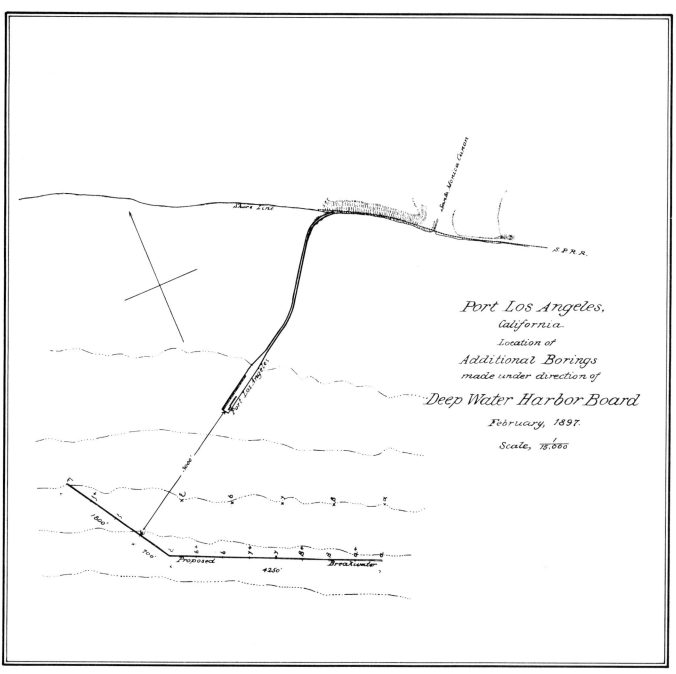

Port Los Angeles,
California.
Location of
Additional Borings
made under direction of
Deep Water Harbor Board
February, 1897.
Scale, $\frac{1}{15,000}$

During its extensive investigations the Walker Board resurveyed and made additional borings at the proposed Port Los Angeles breakwater location.

ately. He ignored this, on the grounds that it had not been passed by the House of Representatives as well. Next, citizens of Los Angeles sent a petition to then President McKinley setting forth the problem and requesting executive action. The President referred it to the Attorney General who, in turn, advised Alger that there were no legal obstacles in the way of his advertising for bids. This written opinion lay on the Secretary's desk for over a month before it was released, in spite of repeated inquiries made of him during that time.

By October of 1897 the General was explaining to critics that his hands were tied because there had been no direct appropriation and he must wait for Congress to vote one. Los Angeles retorted that even if his point were correct, it didn't prevent him

from advertising for bids. The General said that no money was available to pay for such advertisements. Thereupon, the Los Angeles Chamber of Commerce guaranteed payment of all advertising expenses and the newspapers of both San Francisco and Los Angeles volunteered to print them free of charge. The Secretary said that that would not be dignified, and added that he was seeking an opinion

The first load of rock for the breakwater at San Pedro, on its way to be dumped into the sea off Point Fermin.

THE SAN PEDRO DEEP-WATER HARBOR AS IT WILL LOOK WHEN COMPLETED.
(1) **Point Fermin.** (2) **San Pedro.** (3) **Terminal Island.** (4) **Long Beach.** (5) **Los Angeles.** (6) **Wilmington.** (7) **Terminal Railway.**

Artist's conception of how San Pedro Harbor would look when it was completed was published during the harbor battle.

from General McKenna, the Judge Advocate General, which was puzzling since the duties of the latter were purely military in scope.

Nevertheless, General McKenna did issue an opinion, to the effect that there was $50,000 available for advertising purposes. Not long afterward, however, he was appointed to the Supreme Court. Secretary Alger took advantage of that turn of events by resubmitting the question to McKenna's successor as Judge Advocate General, John W. Griggs. At this Los Angeles complained so bitterly to President McKinley that the latter himself instructed Alger to proceed at once.

To this directive the Secretary paid heed. Bids were opened in February 1898, almost a year after the Walker Board's decision. But four more months were to pass before the War Department's engineering authorities filed their report on those bids. It was not until July 21, 1898 that the Secretary of War got around to approving a bid and drawing up a contract, and not until April 16, 1899 that President McKinley pressed a button at the White House which activated the car that dumped the first load of stone for the San Pedro breakwater.

Senator Stephen White died in February 1901 at the early age of 48, without having seen much progress in the construction of the deep-water harbor at San Pedro for which he had eventually fought so well. Although he had been a Democrat, the staunchly Republican *Los Angeles Times* eulogized him as "the greatest man the State has produced in the half century of its existence." Some $25,000 was raised by admiring and grateful citizens to cast his statue in bronze. This monument stood for many years in front of the old brownstone Court House on North Broadway, between First and Temple Streets. When the new Court House was built the statue was moved, and it now stands at the corner of First and Hill Streets, facing the harbor at San Pedro.

Souvenir button issued during the two-day celebration of the "Free Harbor" victory.

Ernest Marquez Collection

Terminal Island about 1899, as viewed from San Pedro. In the foreground is the steamer *Hermosa*. Across the channel are the four-masted barkentine *Willie Hume* and a two-masted schooner, both docked at the pier.

Statue of Senator Stephen M. White.

Donald Duke Collection

91

From 1893, the year in which the Long Wharf was completed, to 1896, the year in which Senator White defeated the Huntington lobby, a total of 759 ships from all parts of the world called at Port Los Angeles. Of these, 52 were sailing vessels and 707 were powered by steam. Two warships were among them, the British man-o'-war *Royal Arthur* on December 29, 1893 and the United States man-o'-war *Monterey* on August 15, 1895, on her way home from a visit to Peru. The latter remained anchored near the wharf for four days, during which the *Collis,* loaded with sightseers, plied back and forth from ship to pier.

The U.S.S. *Monterey* was a coast defense monitor built in 1893. She was 256 feet long, 59 feet wide, had a displacement tonnage of over 4,000, and a freeboard of only three feet. Her biggest guns, "Big Betsey" and "Alice," weighed 50 tons each, and it cost just $533.35 to fire one of them. Visitors

The British ship *Royal Arthur* was a heavily armed cruiser, plated with armor, built in England in 1891. She was 360 feet long and could do 18.5 knots at sea.

Virginia Whippo Collection

92

to the ship were treated to the sight of monkeys and parrots galore which crew members were carrying back from South America. After taking on coal from the Long Wharf, she left for the navy yard at Mare Island to go into dry dock.

On March 2, 1896, some months before the Walker Board arrived in Southern California, one of the worst storms ever to hit Port Los Angeles caused severe damage to the wharf and to the English ship *Dunboyne*. At the time, the *Dunboyne* was tied up on the south side, having already unloaded her cargo of 1,972 tons of cement. The day before, a strong southwest wind had come up and heavy swells developed. Toward midnight the wind shifted to the northeast, a light rain began to fall, and the weather turned cold and raw. The next morning dawned misty, with the wind still blowing northeast.

Captain Dornfield, who supervised operations at the wharf and was in charge of the *Collis,* consulted

The double-turreted monitor *U.S.S. Monterey* at Port Los Angeles. This ship could travel at a speed of about 10 knots and, when underway, raised a heavy wave that covered her bow with water.

The *Alexander Duncan* at Port Los Angeles. Wood,
propellor type, 371 tons, built in 1875 by
Dickie Bros., San Francisco. Acquired by the
Pacific Coast Steamship Company in 1880 and
converted to a coal barge. Broken up in 1916.

Pacific Coast Steamship Company's *Corona*, leaving
Port Los Angeles.

Robert Weinstein Collection

with Captain O'Neil of the *Dunboyne* as to the heavy weather and whether or not he wanted his ship towed away. They decided that if the weather did not clear during the day, they would move her before nightfall. Dornfield was prepared for any emergency and had a fireman and two deckhands standing by on board the tug. Towards noon the storm worsened and the wind was hauling at the ship from the east and southeast. Captain O'Neil concluded she should be towed away from the wharf at once, as she was battering against it and being damaged herself in the process.

Accordingly, they got a hawser onto the *Dunboyne* from the *Collis,* so the tug could pull her out of range of the wharf. Suddenly the wind shifted to the southward and a violent squall produced a heavy swell. The crew of the *Dunboyne* immediately let go the head and stern lines which were

holding the ship to the wharf, but held on to the breast lines attached to the side buoys so they could heave the vessel out as the *Collis* tried to haul her ahead and away from the wharf.

Although the powerful tug was under full steam (115 pounds), she was not able to work the ship broadside to the wind and the heavy sea. The swells were so big that they would throw the stern of the *Collis* out of the water, causing her propeller to race and thereby losing her what little advantage she had gained. Fortunately, the *Corona*, a passenger ship of the Pacific Coast Steamship Company, came along about this time, and since the possibility of the tug's being able to get the *Dunboyne* away from the wharf seemed slight, the two Captains asked the *Corona* to help.

Much time was then wasted trying in vain to get a line from the *Corona* to the *Collis*. Eventually it was decided that the *Corona* should anchor to the windward of the buoys, and after several unsuccessful tries she finally got her anchor off the forecastle deck. A large wharf boat was sent out to her, and it carried an eight-inch line back to the *Collis*.

95

During all this frantic activity the sea had been steadily increasing, so that the *Dunboyne* was now rolling and pitching and slamming the wharf with every swell. Just as the *Corona* and *Collis* were ready to try together to tow her away, the steel hawser from the *Dunboyne* to the after buoy parted about 50 feet from the buoy. As a result, the strain on the English ship was released, and she immediately forged ahead and was easily towed clear of the wharf.

Damage to the wharf consisted of 19 broken fender battens. Damage to the ship *Dunboyne* was described as follows by Captain Dornfield and Agent Jamison:

Starboard topgallant bulwark bent inward for about 25 feet, which necessitates taking off the plate to the sheer strake and having plate re-rolled. Liguum vitae main pin rail back of above-mentioned plate split so that it will have to be removed up to scarf. Starboard cathead torn out of angle irons holding it so that it had to be completely removed in order to replace.

Two deadlights, two half ports, main sheet bolt, and two gangway bolts on starboard side damaged so that they had to be removed.

Port quarter pipe at break of poop cracked. Starboard bulwarks at break of poop slightly bent inward. Main brace, topsail runner, and main brace pennant carried away. Two stanchions supporting main starboard bulwarks bent. Damage to bulwarks at break of poop but slight, and captain agreed to make no mention of it.

The incident was of course brought up at the subsequent hearings of the Walker Board. The *Collis* had suffered a broken propeller, and Captain Dornfield maintained that this was the probable cause of her loss of power and inability to get the

The *Guy C. Goss*, built in Bath, Maine, was the largest wooden three-masted bark launched in the United States. It was employed by the Western Division of the Southern Pacific Railroad to bring coal from Namaino, British Columbia and railroad ties from ports in the Puget Sound. At far left, behind the bigger ship's stern, is the tug *Collis*.

BARK GUY C. GOSS, FROM NEW YORK, APPROACHING S.P. MAMMOTH WHARF, PORT LOS ANGELES, CAL, DEC. 29. 1896.

Dunboyne away from the wharf. Port Los Angeles spokesmen vehemently insisted that for no more than ten days out of an entire year might there be weather in which a ship could not tie up safely at the wharf, and that once a breakwater was built the problem of heavy swells would be completely eliminated. Such explanations did not hinder the opposition from milking the event for all it was worth.

In 1899, the year construction began on the San Pedro breakwater, a Japanese fisherman named Hatsuji Sano, who had come to California from Japan the year before, arrived at Port Los Angeles from Mendocino County in northern California where he had tried unsuccessfully to cultivate abalone. He became the first resident of what grew into a Japanese fishing village north of the Long Wharf. Over the next 10 years the village prospered, and became a desirable summer vacation spot for Los Angeles' Japanese population. In 1909, to take advantage of this trade, a beach resort hotel known as the "Rako Kan" was opened by Kichiro Waseda in Santa Monica Canyon, and in 1911, in the fishing village itself, Hatsuji Sano opened the "Boyo Kan" (Seaview Inn). Although a few Russian fishermen and their families also came to live in the village, it was predominantly Japanese in character, so much so that movies calling for a Japanese setting were sometimes filmed there.

The village's approximately 300 permanent residents, who leased land from the railroad and built their own houses on it, continued to depend upon commercial fishing for their livelihood and operated about 30 boats every day. These boats were valued at about $2,000 apiece, and were individually owned, sometimes two or three by one family. Most of the fishing was done in Santa Monica Bay. Small fish were caught in nets, but large ones, such

The "Japanese Fishing Village," which also served as a resort for Japanese vacationers from Los Angeles, was located on the north side of the Long Wharf.

（スルゼンリーロトーポ）　　館　洋　望

経営者　佐野　初次氏

室内清潔、食事美味、海水浴、温浴萬事に便なり。

君は千葉縣、安房郡、長尾村の人にして明治卅一年渡米せられ加州メンドシノ郡にて鮑事業に従事し居りしが翌卅二年鮑視察の爲め當地に来り鮑業の望なきを悟り獨立にて漁業を開始せらる、これぞ實にポートローサンゼルス漁業者の開祖にして爾来十二年間種々の困難と白人同業者の迫害と戦ひ今日の如き完全なる日本漁村の建築を見るに至る、氏は羅府地方同胞の避暑地の必要なるを悟り同年上岡の如き大館を建築し同胞の宿泊に供す。

Hotel Bōyō, Port Los Angeles, Cal.

P. O. Box 142, Santa Monica, Cal.　　Phone, S.S. Main 168 W 3.

Los Angeles County Museum of Natural History

In 1911 this advertisement for the Boyo Kan Hotel appeared in a Japanese publication. The Japanese text translates as follows:

Top of Page: Port Los Angeles Boyo Kan (sea view hotel)

Left side: Came to Mendocino, California, from Nagao Village, Chiba Prefecture, in 1898 and engaged in abalone fishing. In 1899 came to Port Los Angeles after seeing no future in abalone industry, to start fishing on his own. He is the originator of fishing industry of Port Los Angeles. Fighting persecutions from white fishermen, he successfully built up the Japanese fishing village. He recognized needs for recreational place for the Japanese people of Los Angeles, thus opened this Hotel.

Right Side: First line next to picture — Clean rooms, excellent food, convenient for swimming, hot bath, etc. Last line — Proprietor Mr. Hatsuji Sano

Japanese Free Mii Church (Jiyu Mee-ee). A
Methodist Mission, possibly the beginning of
the Japanese Christian church in Los Angeles.
Sign at left reads: Sunday — 10 A.M. Sunday
School, 7 P.M. Sermon. Wednesday — 7 P.M.
Prayer Meeting. Pastor — Miss Ann Mief.
(Translation is not clear on this name.
Possibly Anmief was the pastor's surname.)

Movie making at the fishing village about 1914.
Japanese movies were made in the Los Angeles
area by a local Japanese company and then sent
to Japan. Sessue Hayakawa was one of several
stars who appeared in these early films.

Prominent Japanese families visited the fishing
village. Pictured above are Mrs. George Bungoro
Tani and her children. Mr. Tani was one of the
major Los Angeles producers of bamboo furniture.
In 1907 he opened the International Theatre in
"Little Tokyo."

as yellowtail, albacore, halibut, and barricuda, were caught with live bait. The albacore ran from 16 to 18 pounds in weight and tuna, of which there was an abundance, ranged from 25 to 30 pounds. As much as 30 tons of fish might be taken in a day, and a "poor day's catch" was anything less than 500 pounds. The Long Wharf served as a landing platform on which to unload the fish, which were then boxed and transported to market.

Severe storms were a menace to these fishermen. Four of the Russians, who had been fishing near the Santa Barbara Islands, were lost for days after such a heavy storm. High tides, too, posed a recurring problem for most of their houses were built directly on the sand, and water would surround and enter them. Many a time valuables and bedding had to be moved to higher ground until the tide retreated.

Collis P. Huntington died on August 13, 1900. The directors of the Southern Pacific elected Charles M. Hays President of the company, but it was E. H. Harriman, another powerful railroad magnate, who took control as Chairman of the Executive Committee. Collis Huntington's nephew Henry, who had wanted to be president, was made a vice-president instead, and he never did achieve the higher position.

In 1902 Harriman himself assumed the title of President of the Southern Pacific. He was unenthusiastic about the Long Wharf, because of its poor profit potential and also because two years before all of the railroads radiating out of the Los Angeles region had begun a general conversion from coal to oil, as a result of which the immense coal bunker was becoming less and less an outstanding asset. Now added to these considerations in his assessment of Port Los Angeles was the fact that the Long Wharf had begun to require expensive maintenance.

Actually, the problem of Port Los Angeles must have been an insignificant one to E. H. Harriman by comparison with the myriad other concerns he confronted daily as a result of the vast railroad empire already under his control, which included the Union Pacific Railroad and numerous other rail lines in the United States, plus investments running into the hundreds of millions of dollars. It seems probable that he lost little if any sleep over the

About 1915 the fishing village was populated by some 300 Japanese residents. Behind their houses lie the Southern Pacific railroad tracks, no longer in use and covered with dirt. The poles with overhead wire for trolleys indicate that at one time the electric cars must have run to some point beyond the Long Wharf.

Los Angeles County Museum of Natural History

S.P.A R. 65879

Robert Weinstein Collection

Looking shoreward toward Santa Monica Canyon
from a three-masted sailing ship docked on the
south side of Port Los Angeles. Ships of this
type carried coal, lumber, and other merchandise
from all parts of the world.

By the turn of the century the time was rapidly
approaching when sailing ships would discontinue
their stops at the Long Wharf and local
residents would no longer be employed there
loading and unloading vessels. Posing on the
ship *Lucipara* from Glasgow, November 28, 1900
are: Top row, 3rd from left, Roman Marquez;
5th, Chucuraco Rivas; 7th, Joe Mariscal;
8th, Leandro Duron; 9th, Mike Duron. Standing
in middle row, 2nd from left, Emilio Lesama;
5th, Frank Garcia; 6th, Frank Marquez;
7th, Estevan de la Pena; 10th, Vincent
Carrillo. Second from left, foreground, Nacho
Rivera. Men not identified are unknown to the
author.

Steamer trunks being loaded onto the *Corona*
at Port Los Angeles in the early 1900's.

Long Wharf and its future, and it is not surprising that a rumor began to spread that the Southern Pacific was planning to abandon it.

In the year 1903 some 283 ships of all types called at the Long Wharf. The Pacific Coast Steamship Company's passenger steamers *Santa Rosa* and *Corona* still made regular calls twice a week southbound from San Francisco and twice a week when northbound. The northbound vessel would arrive at 5:45 A.M. from Redondo and leave for San Francisco at 2.30 P.M. The one-way rate was $12.50 first class, or $8.35 second class. A round trip ticket cost $22.50 and included meals and 150 pounds of free baggage. Over its rival Redondo, Port Los Angeles offered the advantage that passengers going north from Los Angeles could take a much later train from the city in the morning and still make the northbound ship before it left the Long Wharf.

In addition to passenger steamers, steam colliers from Australia and British Columbia, lumber vessels from up the coast, and occasionally a full-rigged sailing ship from Europe docked at Port Los Angeles in the early 1900's. Inevitably, however, in the face of San Pedro's at last incontrovertible

selection, business at the Long Wharf continued to decline. Los Angeles merchants gradually deserted that installation in favor of Congress' and, it might be said, the people's choice for an official harbor for their city.

In 1908 the Southern Pacific, whose locomotives were by then no longer traveling to Port Los Angeles, leased the Long Wharf to the Los Angeles Pacific, which would operate it for the next three years. The Los Angeles Pacific was an electric railway system developed by General Moses H. Sherman and his brother-in-law E. P. Clark, over half the stock of which was owned by the Southern Pacific. The Southern Pacific leased to it the former

Soon after the Los Angeles Pacific Railroad leased the Long Wharf from the Southern Pacific in 1908, poles were erected and the line was electrified. Trolley cars made regularly scheduled round trip runs from Los Angeles to Port Los Angeles.

Tunnel under Ocean Avenue, electrified for the trolleys. The Santa Monica Freeway now passes through this location.

Carl Blaubach Collection

Carl Blaubach Collection

107

Los Angeles & Independence Railroad line from the Sentous Yard (near Culver City) to Santa Monica proper as well as its Port Los Angeles tracks from Santa Monica along the beach to the end of the wharf. The Los Angeles Pacific then erected poles, strung wire, and electrified the entire line all the way out to the end of the Long Wharf.

This marked the beginning of regular electric trolley runs from Los Angeles (via Santa Monica) to the end of the wharf. The wharf became one of the stops on the then famous Balloon Route Excursion Trolley Trips, and the ride out on it was advertised as "an ocean voyage on wheels; an ocean ride without seasickness." Rolling almost a mile out over the ocean on a trolley car was doubtless a memorable experience for many a tourist.

The year 1908 was also the last in which Port Los Angeles appeared on the schedules of the Pacific Coast Steamship Company. After that the big steamers no longer called there.

In 1909 the popular trolley from Santa Monica to the end of the wharf ran every 30 minutes. It took 10 minutes to make the trip. The first car of the day left Santa Monica at 6:40 A.M., and the last one back left the wharf at 10:55 P.M. Extra cars were added on Sundays and holidays to handle the larger crowds. The fare from Los Angeles to the end of the Long Wharf was 35 cents, but it cost only 10 cents to ride out there from Santa Monica.

In May 1910 Sherman and Clark, the developers of the Los Angeles Pacific, retired and sold their remaining stock to the Southern Pacific, thus placing the Southern Pacific in complete control of that electric railway. In December of the same year Los Angeles Pacific officials notified local lumber shippers using Port Los Angeles that they would have to arrange for their cargoes to be handled elsewhere, because in 45 days all shipments via the Long Wharf would be discontinued. The reason given was that maintenance costs for the wharf were so high that it did not pay to keep it in repair. The Southern Pacific announced that its own lumber shipments would subsequently be handled through San Pedro. This marked the end of Port Los Angeles as a port of entry for ocean going vessels.

Repairs to the Long Wharf were indeed badly needed, and at about this time some of its piles

Ticket good for one round trip between Los Angeles and Port Los Angeles.

Los Angeles Pacific Co.
ELECTRIC RAILWAY

1909

The Shortest and Quickest Line between Los Angeles and the Ocean

TO SANTA MONICA, OCEAN PARK, VENICE, REDONDO BEACH, SOLDIERS' HOME, SAWTELLE, SHERMAN, HOLLYWOOD AND COLEGROVE.

LONG WHARF, PORT LOS ANGELES
"As seen on the Balloon Route Excursion"

BALLOON ROUTE EXCURSIONS
ONE WHOLE DAY FOR ONE DOLLAR
101 MILES FOR 100 CENTS

Showing some of California's finest scenery including 36 miles right along the ocean. A reserved seat for every patron and an experienced guide with each car.

The Only Electric Line Excursion Out of Los Angeles Going One Way and Returning Another

FREE ATTRACTIONS: AN OCEAN VOYAGE on Wheels—The Excursion cars running a full mile into the ocean on LONG WHARF, Port Los Angeles; Free admission to the $20,000 AQUARIUM at Venice and a free ride on the ROLLER COASTER at Ocean Park.

Cars leave Hill Street Station, between Fourth and Fifth, LOS ANGELES, at 9:40 A. M. DAILY.

A souvenir button showing the Long Wharf was issued to each tourist who took the "Excursion" trolley trip.

Jeffrey Moreau Collection

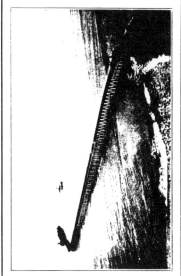

By 1910 Port Los Angeles, no longer used as a port of entry, often stood silent and abandoned. The only activities at that time were occasional shipments of lumber for local merchants or the Southern Pacific and the regularly scheduled trolley trips that brought tourists to see the slowly decaying structure.

As locomotives converted from coal to oil consumption, the great bunker on the Long Wharf ceased to represent a major asset and in 1913 it was dismantled.

Ernest Marquez Collection

were replaced. But such work was halted when an estimate revealed that to put the wharf completely back in shape would cost some $25,000. What exactly was going to happen to the structure became a popular subject for speculation. Its owners did not discuss their plans, and rumors that the wharf was to be destroyed spread unchecked.

On July 13, 1911 a landslide just north of Santa Monica Canyon covered the trolley tracks in the vicinity. Tons of dirt had fallen, and although five men were put to work clearing the tracks, it was some time before trolleys could again go past the Canyon and out onto the wharf.

Shortly after the Southern Pacific came into complete control of the Los Angeles Pacific in 1910 its directors began to pressure Henry Huntington to sell them his remaining half interest in the Pacific Electric Railway, still another electric transportation system, in whose development he had played a key role. An agreement was finally reached the following year, which included a cash bonus to Henry Huntington for agreeing to sell which ran to eight figures. The way was then clear for the Southern Pacific to merge all the numerous Southern California interurban electric railway holdings it had been accumulating.

Such a consolidation took place in September 1911. Its result was the creation of a single corporation named the Pacific Electric Railway Company. This new company now assumed control of the Long Wharf and the property surrounding it, and after the merger the run to the wharf became a section of what was called the Santa Monica Air Line route, part of a mammoth interurban electric system whose lines extended into almost every city and town in Los Angeles and Orange Counties.

Two years later, on September 13, 1913, the Pacific Electric announced that the Port Los Angeles depot building and coal bunker were to be pulled

F. E. Bundy's Bath House was opened on August 1, 1915 and the Pacific Electric cars made regular stops there before heading out onto the Long Wharf. This photograph, taken about 1918, shows Mabery Road and Ocean Way — sidewalks completed but road unpaved. The two-story apartment house and the house next door on Channel Road, the small building directly across the street, and the brick structure on the far right (The Butterfly Inn) are still standing today.

down and the last 1,600 feet of the Long Wharf dismantled. The contract was awarded to August Stutzer, a well-known Santa Monica contractor who had previously built the Municipal Pier at Santa Monica proper, the Mier Pier at Venice, and the wharfs and dykes at Playa del Rey. H. G. Feraud was put in charge of the sale of materials removed from the wharf. It was estimated that the entire job would take about six months to complete. The 3,120 feet of the approach to the wharf was to be retained, however, and maintained as a fishing pier.

The reference source for the above information was the *Santa Monica Daily Outlook* for Saturday, September 13, 1913. The paper devoted one short column to it, and then printed nothing in any subsequent issues about the dismantling of the Long Wharf. One can only conclude that Port Los Angeles, well into its decline, was no longer considered newsworthy.

Then, too, Santa Monicans may not have been unhappy to see it go. Over the years the town's image of itself had firmed into that of a year-round resort. Plans for amusement piers, bathhouses, and pavilions along the beach were in various stages of completion. The idea of that area's also being occupied by railroad tracks and warehouses was less than attractive. As time passed even the name Port Los Angeles fell into disuse. The aging structure came to be referred to most frequently as the Long Wharf, and thought of merely as a good spot from which to fish.

Events which in and of themselves were newsworthy did, however, continue occasionally to occur there. On May 2, 1916, for example, a serious fire broke out late at night in the Japanese village, when one of the fishermen fell asleep while smoking fish in his kitchen. Structures belonging to the railroad, two Japanese hotels, and three Japanese-owned dwellings were destroyed. The residents promptly offered to rebuild the railroad's structures, which were actually the shacks that had once housed workers in the days when Port Los Angeles was being built.

Further, in that year and the next landslide activity in the vicinity of the Long Wharf reached epic proportions. On April 2, 1916 people as far as four miles away were roused from early morning slumber by a tremendous explosion, as the cliff just

north of Santa Monica Canyon again gave way, dumping tons of earth down on the trolley tracks. For a distance of 300 feet they were covered with dirt 10 feet deep, and all trolley poles in the path of the slide were broken. Clean-up and repair work represented a risky undertaking, because the landslide had left a hugely indented cliff with a large overhang of dirt which it was feared might fall at any time and upon which the workmen kept a careful eye.

Even after the tracks were cleared, the Pacific Electric, to prevent the possibility of a car's being trapped under tons of dirt or being isolated from the mainland, did not resume the trolley runs to the end of the wharf that were temporarily discontinued when the slide took place. As anticipated, the rest of the cliff fell on August 23, 1916 and tracks were again inundated for some 300 feet.

Such landslides continued to plague the area. On February 22, 1917 the unstable earth of the cliff about 100 yards to the south of the Long Wharf gave way, covering the tracks with two or three feet of dirt. And on April 4, 1917 the remainder of that bluff fell with a roar heard for miles around. This time 80 laborers were put to work with scrapers and shovels, and two weeks later trolley runs out to the end of the wharf had resumed.

On April 23, 1917 a car leaving the wharf loaded with boxes of fish brought in by the Japanese fishermen bumped over the switches located near Santa Monica Canyon. As it did so, a good-sized fish bounced out of a box onto the floor, from where it dropped out the open door of the car to the track beneath. As chance would have it, the fish landed right in the "mouth" of a switch frog. An hour later, as the wheel of the next car to come by hit the switch, the car was hurled from the tracks and its front rammed into the bank of the palisades. Fortunately, there were no passengers aboard and the damage amounted to no more than a broken step; but since the car had landed at a 45 degree angle to the tracks, a wrecking derrick had to be sent out to lift it back onto them.

Fishing had by that time become the only major activity on the Long Wharf. At the bait house run by R. A. Muller several hundred fishing poles and tackle were available for rent to the public. On August 17, 1917 a sensation was created when the

About 1916: The Long Wharf, reduced to half its
original length, is primarily a fishing pier.
Trolleys were still making regular runs to the
site. Highway below Santa Monica has been
paved as far north as Santa Monica Canyon.

biggest halibut to be caught in several years was taken. It weighed 62¾ pounds, measured 4 feet 2 inches across the back and 5 feet 8 inches from its snout to the end of its tail, and was 40 minutes in the catching.

For the next three years no events of any consequence occurred at the once famous facility. Because World War I was in progress copper wire had become extremely scarce and the Pacific Electric Railway took down the overhead feeder wires in the Japanese village and along tracks that were no longer in use to prevent their being stolen. As a matter of fact, many of the Japanese families had already followed the commercial exodus and moved to a new settlement on Terminal Island, where an all-Japanese village developed at Fish Harbor. Thus did the day approach when the Long Wharf would no longer exist.

On July 9, 1920 the vice-president of the Pacific Electric Railway Company approved the following work order:

Santa Monica, California—Santa Monica Air Line —(leased lines) Western Division—Abandon Air Line from engineer's station 469+91.7 to 506+ 70.5 including Long Wharf, all tracks thereon, 10 bunk houses and one small tool house, bait house, fish loading platform, pipeline and water meters installed in Japanese Village, overhead and bonding. Long Wharf, bunk houses and tool house to be removed are the property of the Southern Pacific Company which company will arrange to retire from its books the ledger value of its property while Pacific Electric Railway Company will bear the expense of removal and deliver salvage material to Southern Pacific Company. Pipeline, bonding, overhead, water systems, telephone and lights are Pacific Electric property and will be retired by it at its expense and book value written off. Detailed estimate attached.

At the bottom of the order the reasons why the Long Wharf was being abandoned were duly set forth:

It is recommended that this portion of the Santa Monica Air Line in the vicinity of Port Los Angeles be abandoned including the Long Wharf as the present condition of the wharf is such that it will require the expenditure of approximately $7,000 for maintenance during the summer; also

Ernest Marquez Collection

116

In the early 1930's the only evidence of the
Long Wharf was the point of land where the huge
structure began. One set of tracks covered
completely by landslides was never uncovered
and the other, partially covered with dirt, was
by this time overgrown with weeds. The "Japanese
Fishing Village" has been razed.

health authorities have ruled that it is absolutely necessary that we install a sewer system for the use of the Japanese Village at an estimated expense of $2,500. The total revenue per annum derived from this portion of the line including the Long Wharf is $11,251 and this does not justify the maintaining of tracks and the wharf when the total operating expense, taxes, etc., exceed the revenue by approximately $4,000 per year; furthermore is the possibility the Japanese Village being declared a nuisance by the City of Santa Monica at any time and in the interest of economy it is considered an opportune time to abandon this portion of the line.

With such prosaic language did "sound business" keep to its course, bestowing not so much as a backward glance on what had been not only a superior installation in its time, but also a noteworthy source of human enjoyment.

Within a month J. D. Keene, the contractor who had been assigned to the dismantling, began the work. As it progressed he announced that the piles were still in good shape and sturdily supporting the wharf. Those salvaged would be used for new piers along the coast, for in spite of their age they were equal to the best new material then available.

By December 1920 Port Los Angeles, after a short but exciting life of 27 years, was no more.

For some time thereafter the Pacific Electric's trolleys continued to run as far as Santa Monica Canyon. In 1924 an hourly service to the Canyon was established, with cars leaving Santa Monica on the hour from 8:00 A.M. to 5:00 P.M. This was maintained for seven years and then, late in 1931, service was reduced to two round trips daily except Sundays. Finally, on August 22, 1933 the Pacific Electric discontinued all trolley service to Santa Monica Canyon. In January of the following year it removed its tracks, poles, and materials from that site, after which the raised area at the mouth of the Canyon was leveled and the trestle dismantled.

For 41 years, from December 31, 1892 until August 22, 1933, the railroad to Port Los Angeles was in continuous use. In this photograph, taken about 1934, the tracks and embankment are being removed from in front of Santa Monica Canyon and two gasoline stations wait in anticipation as the State Highway pushes its way north.

119

Epilogue

I N THE last chapter of *California's Railroad Era* the author, historian Ward McAfee, makes the point that in 1911 "the state had reached the end of an era, characterized by corporate and public disorganization in transportation affairs, and during which community conflicts had played a distinguishing role." In the rise and fall of Senator John P. Jones' Los Angeles & Independence Railroad and Collis P. Huntington's Port Los Angeles, Santa Monica provided the setting for a truly telling example of what he refers to as "the problems and benefits of America's age of unbridled industrial expansion . . . and the complex conditions that gave rise to them."

As for the Long Wharf itself, few other phenomena of such proportions have so soon left so little trace of themselves. Today only a few granite boulders not yet covered by dirt from the landslides that continue to occur and some short lengths of the original railroad track being utilized as parking lot barriers along the beach constitute the sole physical proof that it ever existed.

Ernest Marquez Collection

121

Appendix

The following items are excerpted from the Report
of the Walker Board presented to the United States
Senate on April 1, 1897. Included are lists of
vessels calling at both Port Los Angeles and San
Pedro from 1893 to 1896, arguments for and
against the two sites, and letters from shipmasters
setting forth their views about the Long Wharf.
The Senate and the Engineering Board Reports as
to the selection of Santa Monica or San Pedro as
the location of the deep-water harbor for Los
Angeles are voluminous documents with copious
maps and drawings which deal with the subject in
minute detail.

DEEP-WATER HARBOR.

SAN FRANCISCO, June 11, 1894.

DEAR SIR: Are in receipt of your favor of 9th in re marine rates at San Pedro, Santa Monica, and Redondo. Have seen half a dozen offices on the subject and the consensus of opinion is that on deep-water ships from foreign ports there will be a difference of one-half per cent in favor of San Pedro during the summer months and of at least 1 per cent during the winter months. Two of the companies, in fact, declined to insure deep-water ships at Redondo at all, and the others say that they would prefer not to take the risks. Santa Monica is considered better, but about San Pedro there is no difficulty at all. On steamer rates there is no difference, but on sailing vessels from San Francisco there is a difference of 25 cents during the summer months in favor of San Pedro and of 50 cents during the winter months.

Trusting this will answer your inquiry,

Very truly, yours,

BROWN, CRAIG & CO.

BEN. E. WARD, Esq.,
Los Angeles, Cal.

Freight vessels arriving at Port Los Angeles.

[Exclusive of Pacific Coast Steamship Company's steamers.]

Date.	Name of vessel.	Registered tonnage.	From the port of—	Cargo.
1893.				
May 9	Tug Collis	102	San Francisco	4,200 tons coal.
11	Steamer San Mateo	1,926	Comax	4,300 tons coal.
June 1	...do	1,926	Comax	
9	Tug Collis	102	San Francisco	5,720 ties.
13	Steamer Newsboy	150	Navarro	42,064 feet, B.M. lumber.
15	Steamer Mineola	1,892	New York	700 tons rail; 500 tons merchandise.
17	Ship India	1,230	Nanaimo	4,300 tons coal.
23	Steamer Alcazar	202	Point Arena	2,068 ties.
26	Steamer Alcatraz	193	...do	2,403 ties.
27	Steamer Whitesboro	144	Cleone	6,150 ties.
29	Steamer Westport	154	Bear Harbor	7,680 ties.
30	Steamer Sunol	194	Point Arena	8,169 ties.
July 1	Steamer Alcazar	202	...do	8,341 ties.
5	Steamer Lakme	404	Noyo	9,125 ties.
8	Steamer Alcatraz	193	Cleone	6,240 ties.
10	Steamer Greenwood	144	Noyo	9,400 ties.
10	Steamer Alcatraz	193	Point Arena	6,352 ties.
11	Steamer Whitesboro	144	Comax	4,300 tons coal.
12	Steamer San Mateo	1,926	Point Arena	8,388 ties.
13	Steamer Sunol	194	Eureka	195,000 feet,B.M.,lumber.
14	Steamer Pasadena	235	Navarro	8,200 ties.
16	Steamer Alcazar	202	Cleone	6,603 ties.
17	Steamer Newsboy	150	Navarro	7,860 ties.
18	Steamer Westport	154	Bear Harbor	8,337 ties.
23	Steamer Whitesboro	144	Point Arena	8,160 ties.
23	...do	144	...do	8,664 ties.
24	Steamer Albion	150	Westport	8,689 ties.
24	Schooner M. C. Russ	180	Navarro	8,475 ties.
27	Steamer Sunol	194	Point Arena	8,475 ties.
28	Steamer Alcazar	202	...do	18,139 ties.
28	Steamer Lakme	404	Fort Bragg	30,218 feet, B.M.,lumber; 6,496 ties.
29	Steamer Newsboy	150	Navarro	8,396 ties.
Aug. 3	Steamer Alcatraz	193	Point Arena	3,100 tons coal.
3	Steamer Mineola	1,892	Comax	6,300 ties.
5	Steamer Whitesboro	144	Cleone	8,720 ties.
6	Steamer Alcazar	202	Point Arena	18,664 feet, B.M.,lumber; 7,932 ties.
10	Steamer Hermosa	249	Greenwood	8,095 ties.
12	Steamer Alcatraz	193	Point Arena	6,175 ties.
15	Steamer Whitesboro	144		
17	Steamer Hermosa	249	Cleone	53,480 feet, B.M.,lumber; 6,408 ties.
18	Steamer Greenwood	144		6,480 ties.
25	Steamer Mineola	1,892	...do	8,651 ties.
28	Steamer Greenwood	144	Cleone	3,100 tons coal.
30	Steamer Sunol	194	Point Arena	8,840 ties.

DEEP-WATER HARBOR.

Freight vessels arriving at Port Los Angeles—Continued.

Date.	Name of vessel.	Registered tonnage.	From the port of—	Cargo.
1893.				
Sept. 4	Ship India	1,230	Nanaimo	2,089 tons coal.
16	Steamer Mineola	1,892	Comax	3,100 tons coal.
29	Steamer Caspar	234	Caspar	
29	Tug Pelican	12	Redondo	
Oct. 10	Schooner Bobolink	161	Mendocino	197,428 feet,B.M.,lumber.
15	Steamer Pasadena	202	Via Redondo	162,000 feet,B.M.,lumber.
Nov. 18	Revenue cutter Nymphe	150	Eureka	112,000 feet,B.M.,lumber.
Dec. 1	Steamer McArthur	112	San Francisco	Surveying cruise.
1	Bark Aumliere	1,329	Liverpool	1,200 tons merchandise.
7	Steamer Mineola	1,892	Comax	2,900 tons coal.
29	Man-of-war Royal Arthur	7,700	S. Bar. (England)	None.
30	Steamer San Mateo	1,926	Comax	4,150 tons coal.
1894.				
Jan. 23	Steamer San Mateo	1,926	...do	4,150 tons coal.
Feb. 16	Steamer Mineola	1,892	...do	2,900 tons coal.
16	Schooner J. Wand	163	Eureka	275,000 feet,B.M.,lumber.
19	Schooner H. N. Kimball	182	...do	111,000 feet,B.M.,lumber.
20	Tug Warrior	44	San Pedro	None.
Mar. 12	Steamer San Mateo	1,926	Comax	4,150 tons coal.
12	Steamer Mineola	1,892	...do	2,900 tons coal.
21	Steamer San Mateo	1,926	...do	4,150 tons coal.
Apr. 2	Tug Warrior	44	San Francisco	None.
8	Steamer Wellington	1,267	Comax	2,400 tons coal.
16	Steamer San Mateo	1,926	...do	4,300 tons coal.
26	Steamer Wellington	1,267	...do	2,400 tons coal.
May 17	Steamer Scotia	132	Bowens Landing	6,680 ties.
17	Steamer Wellington	1,267	Dep. Bay	2,360 tons coal.
22	Steamer Sunol	194	Point Arena	8,415 ties.
23	Steamer San Mateo	1,926	Comax	4,300 tons coal.
26	Steamer Alcazar	202	Greenwood	8,423 ties.
29	Steamer Alcatraz	193	Point Arena	8,345 ties.
31	Steamer Protection	216	Whitesboro	9,050 ties.
June 31	Steamer Sunol	194	Point Arena	9,592 ties.
1	Steamer Wellington	1,267	Comax	2,400 tons coal.
12	Steamer Protection	216	Point Arena	9,195 ties.
13	Steamer Alcazar	202	Bowens Landing	8,936 ties.
16	Steamer San Mateo	1,926	Comax	4,300 tons coal.
16	Steamer Alcatraz	193	Point Arena	8,855 ties.
21	Steamer Minetta	150	Albion	698 ties.
21	Steamer Mineola	1,892	Comax	3,100 tons coal.
26	Steamer Alcatraz	193	Point Arena	8,436 ties.
28	Revenue cutter Oliver Wolcott	199	San Diego	None.
July 29	Steamer Sunol	194	Point Arena	8,940 ties.
4	Steamer Alcazar	202	...do	None.
5	Schooner Bobolink	161	Mendocino	Do.
20	Steamer Rawmore	1,438	Payta, Peru	None.
27	Steamer Mineola	1,892	Comax	3,100 tons coal.
27	Schooner Olga	473	Tacoma	604,727 feet,B.M.,lumber.
28	Ship Glencairn	1,500	Antwerp (for Redondo)	None.
29	Steamer Alcazar	202	Greenwood	9,221 ties.
31	Steamer Newsboy	150	Bowens Landing	2,592 ties.
31	Steamer Alcatraz	193	Point Arena	8,560 ties.
Aug. 6	Steamer Mineola	1,892	Comax	3,100 tons coal.
6	Steamer Protection	216	Bowens Landing	8,429 ties.
14	Steamer San Mateo	1,926	Greenwood	10,105 ties.
23	Steamer Mineola	1,892	Comax	3,100 tons coal.
24	Steamer Sunol	194	Greenwood	9,341 ties.
25	Schooner Bobolink	161	Mendocino	85,459 feet, B.M. lumber.
26	Steamer Alcatraz	193	Point Arena	8,724 ties.
Sept. 4	Steamer San Mateo	1,926	Comax	4,300 tons coal.
4	Steamer Protection	216	Bowens Landing	8,668 ties.
4	Steamer Caspar	234	Caspar	350,479 feet,B.M.,lumber.
7	Steamer Alcazar	202	Greenwood	4,619 ties.
7	Steamer Excelsior	364	Ventura	Passenger excursion.
8	Ship Crown of England	1,657		3,329 tons coal.
8	Steamer Mineola	1,892	Comax	3,100 tons coal.
11	Steamer Alcatraz	194	Point Arena	8,427 ties.
13	Steamer Alcazar	202	Point Arena	8,784 ties.
17	Ship Elginshire	2,093	London	89 tons merchandise; 2,240 tons cement.
20	Steamer Sunol	194	Point Arena	9,941 ties.
21	Steamer San Mateo	1,926	Comax	4,300 tons coal.
23	Steamer Alcazar	202	Point Arena	9,120 ties.
26	Steamer Crown of England	1,657	Nanaimo	3,394 tons coal.

Freight vessels arriving at Port Los Angeles—Continued.

Date.	Name of vessel.	Registered tonnage.	From the port of—	Cargo.
1894.				
Sept. 26	Steamer Mineola	1,892	Comax	3,100 tons coal.
Oct. 4	Steamer Alcatraz	193	Greenwood	8,572 ties.
5	Steamer Sunol	194	Point Arena	8,160 ties.
5	Wrecker S. Pedro	100	Redondo	None.
6	Steamer Whitesboro	202	Whitesboro	5,581 ties.
7	Steamer San Mateo	1,926	Comax	4,300 tons coal.
7	Steamer Alcatraz	193	Point Arena	8,961 ties.
13	Ship Jabez Howes	1,581	New York	1,645 tons merchandise; 878 tons coal.
14	Steamer Sunol	194	Point Arena	9,280 ties.
15	Schooner Bobolink	161	Mendocino	194,416 feet,B.M.,lumber.
16	Steamer Tillamook	208	Bowens Landing	8,500 ties.
20	Steamer Alcazar	202	Whitesboro	8,000 ties.
25	Tug Warrior	44	San Pedro	None.
27	Steamer Caspar	234	Caspar	42,611 feet, B.M.,lumber.
Nov. 1	Steamer Alcatraz	193	Point Arena	8,475 ties.
2	Steamer Rival	203	Fort Bragg	200,756 feet,B.M.,lumber.
3	Steamer Sunol	194	Greenwood	8,533 ties.
10	Steamer Alcatraz	193	Point Arena	8,400 ties.
12	Tug Warrior	44	San Pedro	None.
18	...do Alcatraz	193	Point Arena	Do.
18	Tug Warrior	44	Santa Rosa Island	8,400 ties.
27	Steamer Sunol	194	Greenwood	6,553 ties ; 83,060 feet, B.
28	...do	194	...do	None.
28	Steamer Alcatraz	193	Point Arena	9,467 ties.
28	Steamer Mineola	1,892	Comax	8,400 ties.
Dec. 8	Steamer Sunol	194	Whitesboro	3,000 tons coal.
9	Tug Collis	102	San Francisco	None.
10	Steamer Alcatraz	193	Greenwood	8,580 ties.
12	Steamer Jewel	202	Caspar	96,134 feet, B.M., lumber.
19	Steamer Mineola	1,892	Mendocino	3,000 tons coal.
19	Steamer Caspar	234	Whitesboro	315,863 feet,B.M.,lumber.
20	Steamer Alcazar	202	Comax	8,377 ties.
21	Steamer San Mateo	1,926	Comax	4,100 tons coal.
21	Steamer Mineola	1,892	...do	3,000 tons coal.
1895.				
Jan. 9	Steamer San Mateo	1,892	...do	4,100 tons coal.
13	Steamer Mineola	1,892	Tacoma	3,000 tons coal.
15	Steamer Wellington	1,267	Tacoma	2,350 tons coal.
17	Schooner Reporter	333	Fort Bragg	419,000 feet,B.M.,lumber.
29	Steamer Sunol	194	Fort Bragg	4,460 ties.
Feb. 7	Steamer San Mateo	1,926	Comax	1,500 ties.
11	Steamer Tillamook	208	Fort Bragg	18,000 ties.
11	Steamer P. Jebsen	404	Comax	
12	Steamer Lakme	404	...do	4,332 tons coal.
12	Ship Port Stanly	2,187	Greenwood	3,459 tons coal.
12	Steamer Whitesboro	144	Bowens Landing	6,215 ties.
14	Steamer Newsboy	150	Noyo	5,941 ties ; 20,000 feet, B. M., lumber.
21	Steamer Protection	216	Fort Bragg	8,752 ties.
25	Steamer San Mateo	1,926	Comax	4,100 tons coal.
Mar. 1	Steamer Mineola	1,892	...do	3,000 tons coal.
3	Steamer Lakme	404	Fort Bragg	13,000 ties.
3	Steamer Sunol	194	Greenwood	28,700 feet, B.M., lumber; 8,521 ties.
9	Steamer Nat. City	220		5,137 ties.
9	Steamer Mineola	208	Bowens Landing	8,000 ties.
11	Steamer Lakme	404	Fort Bragg	17,312 ties.
11	Steamer Protection	216	Fort Bragg	60,000 feet, B.M., lumber.
13	Steamer San Mateo	194	Comax	7,462 ties.
14	Steamer Mineola	1,892	...do	3,000 tons coal.
16	Steamer Greenwood	144	Greenwood	7,464 ties; 182 piles.
18	Steamer Tillamook	208	Bowens Landing	7,465 ties.
22	Steamer Greenwood	194	Noyo	4,150 ties.
26	Steamer Sunol	194	Greenwood	6,366 ties.
28	Steamer Westport	144	Fort Bragg	226 telegraph poles.
29	Steamer Newsboy	154	Albion	800 ties.
30	Steamer Lakme	404	Fort Bragg	15,000 ties.
Apr. 2	Steamer San Mateo	1,926	Comax	4,100 tons coal.
2	Steamer Alcatraz	193	Greenwood	8,665 ties.
6	Steamer Sunol	194	Fort Bragg	8,800 ties.
7	Steamer Greenwood	144	Fort Bragg	6,129 ties.
11	Steamer Alcazar	202	Greenwood	9,615 ties.
11	Steamer Alcatraz	193	Westport	8,639 ties.
15	Steamer Jewel	202	Navarro	5,500 ties.

DEEP-WATER HARBOR.

Freight vessels arriving at Port Los Angeles—Continued.

Date.	Name of vessel.	Registered tonnage.	From the port of—	Cargo.
1895.				
Apr. 17	Steamer Tillamook	208	Bowens Landing	8,600 ties.
17	Steamer Alcazar	202	Newport	9,000 ties.
19	Steamer San Mateo	1,926	Comax	4,200 tons coal.
21	Steamer Greenwood	144	Bowens Landing	6,050 tons coal.
21	Steamer Whitesboro	144	Greenwood	4,604 ties, 55,753 feet, B. M. lumber.
23	Steamer Sunol	194	...do	8,627 ties.
25	Steamer Jewel	202	Bowens Landing	9,255 ties.
25	Steamer P. Jebsen	404	Nanaimo	4,452 tons coal.
28	Steamer Lakme	2,248	Noyo	16,000 ties.
28	Steamer Alcazar	202	Newport	9,040 ties.
29	Steamer Greenwood	144	Greenwood	6,243 ties.
29	Steamer Protection	216	Usal	42,500 feet, B.M., lumber.
May 2	Schooner Seven Sisters	122	Biehlers Point	5,000 ties.
2	Steamer Alcazar	148	Navarro	5,609 ties.
3	Steamer Sunol	194	Greenwood	8,318 ties ; 17,740 feet, B. M. lumber.
6	Steamer San Mateo	1,926	Comax	4,200 tons coal.
7	Steamer Alcatraz	193	Westport	7,840 ties.
9	Steamer Alcazar	202	Greenwood	9,127 ties.
12	Steamer Mineola	1,892	Comax	3,150 tons coal.
13	Steamer Scotia	132	Bowens Landing	7,700 ties.
17	Steamer Alcatraz	193	Cleone	8,810 ties.
17	Steamer Greenwood	144	Greenwood	2,502 ties ; 28,038 feet, B. M. lumber.
17	Steamer Sunol	194	Point Arena	8,200 ties.
19	Steamer Alcazar	202	Cleone	9,160 ties.
19	Schooner Jos. Russ	235	Seattle	339,952 feet.B.M.lumber.
23	Steamer Nat. City	193	Eureka	220,796 feet,B.M.lumber.
23	Steamer San Mateo	1,928	Comax	4,200 tons coal.
26	Steamer Cleone	194	Point Arena	9,600 ties.
26	Steamer P. Jebsen	140	Usal	126,432 feet,B.M.lumber.
31	Steamer Alcazar	2,248	Nanaimo	4,460 tons coal.
31	Steamer Alcazar	202	Point Arena	6,400 ties ; 60,000 feet, B. M. lumber.
June 24	Steamer Tillamook	208	San Pedro	Put in for coal.
2	Steamer Alcatraz	193	Point Arena	8,383 ties.
3	Steamer Tillamook	208	Bowens Landing	9,050 ties.
3	Schooner Reporter	333	Tacoma	440,347 feet,B.M.lumber.
4	Steamer Sunol	194	Point Arena	9,469 ties.
5	Steamer Mineola	1,892	Comax	3,150 tons coal.
12	Steamer Alcatraz	193	Whitesboro	74,069 feet,B.M.lumber.
12	Steamer Sunol	194	Point Arena	8,709 ties.
13	Steamer Nat. City	1,926	Eureka	110,000 feet,B.M.lumber.
13	Steamer San Mateo	154	Comax	4,200 tons coal.
14	Steamer Westport	148	Bear Harbor	8,400 ties.
17	Schooner P. Miller	2,248	Navarro	5,194 ties.
18	Steamer P. Jebsen	144	Nanaimo	4,470 tons coal.
18	Steamer Greenwood	202	Point Arena	9,100 ties.
21	Steamer Alcazar	193	Cleone	9,100 ties.
22	Steamer Alcatraz	194	Point Arena	8,571 ties.
23	Steamer Alcazar	202	...do	8,484 ties.
30	Steamer Alcazar	193	...do	8,502 ties.
30	Steamer Sunol	220	Greenwood	7,154 ties ; 73,317 feet, B. M. lumber.
July 30	Steamer Nat. City		Eureka	38,830 feet, B.M, lumber.
30	Steamer Sunol	208	Point Arena	8,568 ties.
3	Schooner Caspar	122	Newport	10,160 ties.
3	Schooner Seven Sisters	202	Phelps Landing	4,500 ties.
8	Steamer Jewel	142	Bowens Landing	9,450 ties.
8	Steamer Laguna	193	Bear Harbor	7,500 ties.
8	Steamer Sunol	193	Westport	8,729 ties.
8	Steamer Alcatraz	154	Point Arena	9,200 ties.
11	Steamer Alcazar	203	Cleone	8,860 ties.
13	Steamer Rival	144	Bear Harbor	8,850 ties.
14	Steamer Protection	144	Fort Bragg	9,067 ties.
14	Steamer San Mateo	216	Point Arena	6,245 ties.
16	...do	194	...do	6,200 ties.
16	Steamer Greenwood	202	Westport	9,330 ties.
16	Steamer Protection	144	Whitesboro	8,671 ties.
19	Steamer Alcazar	220	Eureka	27,758 ties. B.M.lumber.
19	Steamer Nat. City	202	Cleone	4,700 ties.
23	Steamer Alcatraz	193	Point Arena	4,844 ties. M. lumber.
28	Steamer Sunol	194	Greenwood	150,081 feet, lumber.
24	Steamer Alcazar	202	Point Arena	8,800 ties.
26	Steamer Jewel	204	Bowens Landing	9,500 ties.
27	Steamer Caspar	193	Newport	10,200 ties.
31	Steamer Alcatraz	193	Point Arena	9,125 ties.
31	Steamer Sunol	194	Whitesboro	9,100 ties.

S. Doc. 18——20

Freight vessels arriving at Port Los Angeles—Continued.

Date.	Name of vessel.	Registered tonnage.	From the port of—	Cargo.
1896.				
July 18	Steamer Caspar	234	Caspar	Put in for telegram.
Aug. 3	Steamer Alcazar	202	Cleone	9,579 ties.
Aug. 3	Ship Eclipse	1,536	New York	347 tons coal; 1,963 tons merchandise.
7	Steamer Westport	154	Needle Rock	6,552 ties.
9	Steamer Caspar	234	Noyo	9,731 ties; 29,634 feet, B. M., lumber.
10	Steamer Sunol	194	Whitesboro	9,000 ties.
11	Steamer Laguna	142	Bear Harbor	3,300 ties.
11	Steamer Alcatraz	193	Point Arena	3,725 ties.
12	Ship Fingal	2,485	Newcastle	3,243 tons coal.
13	Steamer Whitesboro	144	Point Arena	1,854 tons cement.
13	Ship Lady Isabella	1,462	Hamburg	10,623 ties.
14	Steamer Alcazar	202	Needle Rock	7,300 ties.
20	Steamer Cleone	140	Westport	8,600 ties.
21	Steamer Alcatraz	193	Point Arena	5,500 ties; 120,000 feet, B. M., lumber.
21	Steamer Sunol	194	Greenwood	4,500 ties.
29	Schooner Seven Sisters	122	Bichlers Point	9,130 ties.
24	Steamer Alcazar	202	Cleone	9,375 ties.
30	Steamer Jewel	202	Bowens Landing	9,428 ties, 20,136 feet, B. M., lumber.
30	Steamer Sunol	194	Greenwood	10,000 ties.
31	Steamer Alcatraz	198	Needle Rock	To enter custom-house.
19	Schooner E. Claudina	185	Vancouver	
19	Man-of-war Monterey	a3,000	Redondo	
Sept. 9	Steamer Sunol	194	Cleone	8,660 ties.
9	Steamer Mineola	1,892	Comax	3,200 tons coal.
12	Steamer Alcatraz	193	Needle Rock	9,900 ties.
24	Steamer G. W. Watson	430	Tacoma	584,198 feet, B. M., lumber
24	Steamer Mineola	1,892	Comax	3,200 tons coal.
29	Steamer Alcatraz	193	Greenwood	163,641 feet, B.M., lumber; 4,300 ties.
28	Tug Collis	102	San Francisco	None.
Oct. 3	Steamer So. Coast	289	Trinidad	40,000 feet, B.M., lumber.
8	Steamer Mineola	1,892	Comax	3,200 tons coal.
8	Steamer P. Jebsen	2,248	Nanaimo	4,499 tons coal.
11	Steamer Excelsior	364	Eureka	155,000 feet,B.M., lumber.
14	Steamer San Mateo	1,926	Comax	4,200 tons coal.
21	Steamer Alcatraz	193	Point Arena	420,677 feet,B.M.,lumber.
22	Steamer San Mateo	1,926	Comax	4,200 tons coal.
30	Schooner Premier	292	Tacoma	3,430 ties.
30	Steamer San Mateo	1,926	Comax	4,050 tons coal.
Nov. 3	Schooner N. Sundborg	63	Stewarts Point	827,364 feet,B.M.,lumber.
17	Steamer San Mateo	1,926	Comax	448 tons merchandise; 1,120 tons cement.
13	Bark E. Talbot	1,193	Vancouver	552,000 feet,B.M.,lumber.
14	Bark Edinburghire	1,277	London	661 tons merchandise; 1,144 tons cement.
9	Ship Eaton Hall	1,779	...do	108,000 feet,B.M.,lumber.
19	Steamer Alcazar	202	Greenwood	192 tons merchandise; 800 tons cement.
22	Bark Forfarshire	1,300	Antwerp	3,280 tons cement.
2	Steamer Mineola	1,892	Comax	For coal.
2	Steamer Jewel	202	Newport	
2	Steamer yacht Eleanor	a250	San Diego (tour around world)	
Dec. 4	Steamer Mineola	1,892	Comax	3,100 tons coal.
7	Steamer San Mateo	1,926	...do	4,050 tons coal.
8	Schooner O. M. Kellogg	373	Graves Harbor	479,093 feet,B.M.,lumber.
10	Ship Point Elgin	1,628	Newcastle	2,694 tons coal.
14	Steamer Sunol	194	Point Arena	8,150 ties.
14	Steamer Alcatraz	193	Comax	120,872 feet,B.M.,lumber.
16	Steamer Newsboy	150	Usal	4,050 tons coal.
24	Steamer San Mateo	1,926	Comax	92,263 feet,B.M.,lumber.
26	Steamer Alcatraz	193	Point Arena	
1896.				
24	Steamer Alcazar	202	Newport	For coal.
12	Tug Warrior	44	San Pedro	None.
Jan. 3	Steamer Progressist	2,025	Comax	3,700 tons coal.
5	Steamer Alcazar	193	Point Arena	8,500 ties.
8	Steamer Excelsior	364	Eureka	149,813 feet,B.M.,lumber.
12	Steamer P. Jebsen	2,248	Nanaimo	4,287 tons coal.
13	Ship Airlie	1,392	Antwerp	380 tons merchandise, 903 tons cement.
18	Steamer City of Everet	1,858	Panama	No freight.
13	Steamer San Mateo	1,926	Comax	4,050 tons coal.
14	Steamer Alcazar	202	Point Arena	8,240 ties.

a About.

DEEP-WATER HARBOR.

Freight vessels arriving at Port Los Angeles—Continued.

Date.	Name of vessel.	Registered tonnage.	From the port of—	Cargo.
1896.				
Jan. 19	Steamer Progress	1,445	Comax	2,450 tons coal.
Jan. 25	Steamer Alcazar	202	Greenwood	4,029 ties, 155,172 feet, B. M., lumber.
27	Steamer Progressist	2,025	Comax	3,700 tons coal.
28	Steamer Excelsior	364	Albion	56,112 feet, B.M., lumber.
29	Steamer Mineola	1,892	Comax	3,100 tons coal.
30	Steamer Scotia	113	Greenwood	63,163 feet, B.M., lumber.
Feb. 4	Steamer San Mateo	1,926	Comax	4,050 tons coal.
Feb. 10	Ship St. John	1,826	New York	1,484 tons coal; 1,482 tons merchandise.
16	Ship Dunboyne	1,380	London	1,972 tons cement.
20	Steamer Mineola	1,892	Comax	3,100 tons coal.
24	Steamer San Mateo	1,926	...do	4,050 tons coal.
28	Steamer Nat. City	220	Eureka	37,088 feet, B.M., lumber.
28	Steamer Colon	843	Panama	No freight.
Mar. 2	Steamer Mineola	1,892	Comax	3,050 tons coal.
Mar. 3	Ship Philadelphia	1,709	Hamburg	11 tons merchandise; 3,060 tons cement.
13	Steamer Newsboy	150	Usal	145,672 feet,B.M.,lumber.
13	Steamer San Mateo	1,926	Comax	4,050 tons coal.
28	Bark Fernbank	1,338	Antwerp	642 tons merchandise; 848 tons cement.
Apr. 30	Schooner Seven Sisters	122	Bowens Landing	2,010 ties.
Apr. 5	Schooner Sacramento	124	Albion	5,384 ties.
6	Steamer Protection	215	Bowens Landing	9,200 ties; 146 tie poles.
12	Steamer Mineola	1,892	Comax	3,100 tons coal.
23	Ship C. E. Moody	1,915	New York	1,595 tons merchandise, 1,372 tons coal, 150 tons coke.
May 29	Steamer P. Jebsen	2,248	Nanaimo	4,432 tons coal.
30	Steamer San Mateo	1,926	Comax	4,200 tons coal.
May 16	Steamer Alcazar	202	Greenwood	105,496 feet,B.M.,lumber.
18	Steamer P. Jebsen	2,248	Nanaimo	4,348 tons coal.
19	Steamer Westport	154	Bear Harbor	7,440 ties.
30	Steamer Protection	216	Usal	77,701 feet, B.M., lumber.
June 9	Steamer P. Jebsen	2,248	Nanaimo	4,397 tons coal.
14	Steamer Westport	154	Bear Harbor	6,960 ties.
14	Steamer Dunayre	2,056	Newcastle	3,340 tons coal.
22	Steamer Alcazar	202	Greenwood	65,692 feet, B.M., lumber.
24	Steamer P. Jebsen	2,248	Nanaimo	4,421 tons coal.
July 26	Steamer Newsboy	150	Usal	60,887 feet, B.M., lumber.
26	Steamer Alcazar	202	Greenwood	47,152 feet,B.M., lumber.
30	Steamer Westport	154	Bear Harbor	7,920 ties.
12	Steamer P. Jebsen	2,248	Nanaimo	4,415 tons coal.
15	Schooner Alice	220	Fills Landing	330,243 feet,B.M.,lumber.
25	Steamer Lakme	404	Usal	192,111 feet,B.M.,lumber.
29	Bark Gulf Stream	1,378	Antwerp	573,014 feet,B.M.,lumber; 822 tons cement; 256 tons merchandise.
Aug. 3	Schooner Reporter	333	Everett	552,000 feet,B.M.,lumber.
Aug. 4	Ship Drumcliff	2,468	London	228 tons coke, 1,175 tons cement, 981 tons merchandise.
11	Bark Artemis	1,407	Hamburg	1,246 tons cement; 6 tons merchandise.
18	Steamer Protection	216	Usal	57,431 feet, B.M., lumber.
24	Steamer Alcazar	202	Greenwood	252,367 feet,B.M., lumber.
Sept. 10	Steamer Mineola	1,892	Comax	3,200 tons coal.
24	Steamer Protection	216	Usal via Redondo	138,471 feet, B.M., lumber.
24	Steamer P. Jebsen	2,248	Nanaimo	4,435 tons coal.
Oct. 18	Steamer Nat. City	220	Eureka	78,610 feet, B.M., lumber.
18	Steamer Mineola	1,892	Comax	4,487 tons coal.
26	Steamer P. Jebsen	2,248	Nanaimo	4,100 tons coal.
Nov. 21	Steamer W'schtenan	2,004	Comax	4,150 tons coal.
21	Steamer Mineola	1,892	...do	4,150 tons coal.
28	Steamer Newsboy	150	Hardy Creek	2,904 ties.
28	Steamer Mineola	1,892	Comax	3,050 tons coal.
Dec. 10	Schooner Ethel Zane	473	Port Gamble	100,000 feet,B.M.,lumber.
Dec. 10	Port Crawford	1,598	Hamburg	2,380 tons cement.
	J. C. Goss	1,524		50 tons iron.

DEEP-WATER HARBOR.

RECAPITULATION.

May 9 to Dec. 31, 1893:

Coal	tons..	33,307
Ties	do..	272,387
Lumber	feet, B. M..	990,852
New York and foreign vessels—		
1 steamer from New York—		
Rails	tons..	700
Merchandise	do..	500
1 bark from Liverpool, merchandise	do..	1,200

Jan. 1 to Dec. 31, 1894:

Coal	do..	96,333
Ties	do..	354,179
Lumber	feet, B. M.,	2,359,505
New York and foreign vessels—		
1 ship from London—		
Merchandise	tons..	89
Cement	do..	2,240
1 ship from New York—		
Cement	do..	1,645
Merchandise	do..	878

Jan. 1 to Dec. 31, 1895:

Coal	do..	117,102
Ties	do..	659,189
Lumber	feet, B. M.,	5,491,147
Piles	do..	182
Telegraph poles	do..	226
New York and foreign vessels, coal		
3 ships from Newcastle, coal		10,038
1 ship from New York—		
Coal	do..	347
Merchandise	do..	1,963
1 ship from Hamburg, cement	do..	1,854
1 bark from Antwerp—		
Merchandise	do..	192
Cement	do..	800
1 bark from London—		
Merchandise	do..	448
Cement	do..	1,120
1 ship from London—		
Merchandise	do..	661
Cement	do..	1,144

DEEP-WATER HARBOR.

Los Angeles and ocean traffic September 1, 1895, to August 31, 1896.

NORTH AND SOUTH BOUND.

	Pounds.	Per cent.
Port Los Angeles	32,415,615	49.8
San Pedro	3,059,850	4.6
East San Pedro	5,680,738	8.7
Southern California Railway } Redondo.	11,789,507	17.9
Redondo Railway	12,832,600	19.5
Total	65,758,310	....

Each port.

	Pounds.	Per cent.
Port Los Angeles	32,415,615	49.3
San Pedro	} 8,720,588	13.3
East San Pedro		
Redondo	24,022,107	37.4

Each company.

	Pounds.	Per cent.
Port Los Angeles	35,455,465	53.9
San Pedro	5,680,738	8.7
East San Pedro	11,789,507	17.9
Southern California Railway		
Redondo Railway	12,832,600	19.5

	North bound.		South bound.	
	Pounds.	Per cent.	Pounds.	Per cent.
Port Los Angeles	2,383,050	43.5	30,032,565	49.8
San Pedro	741,490	13.6	2,297,960	3.8
East San Pedro	526,290	9.6	5,114,448	8.6
Southern California Railway	1,573,818	28.7	10,215,689	16.9
Redondo Railway	251,542	4.6	12,381,058	20.9
Total	5,476,590		60,281,720	

Each port.

	North bound.		South bound.	
	Pounds.	Per cent.	Pounds.	Per cent.
Port Los Angeles		43.5		49.8
San Pedro	}	23.2		12.4
East San Pedro				
Redondo		33.3		37.8

Each company.

	North bound.		South bound.	
	Pounds.	Per cent.	Pounds.	Per cent.
Port Los Angeles		57.1		53.6
San Pedro		9.6		8.6
East San Pedro		28.7		16.9
Southern California Railway				
Redondo Railway		4.6		20.9

EXHIBIT NO. 6.

LOS ANGELES, CAL., *December 17, 1896.*

DEAR SIR: Inclosed please find a statement of Los Angeles tonnage, both north and south bound, handled at the different ports for twelve months ending August 31, 1896.

You will notice that there are four wharves at which Los Angeles freight, in connection with the Pacific Coast Steamship Company, is handled—Port Los Angeles, San Pedro, East San Pedro, and Redondo—and that of the total tonnage, 65,758,310 pounds, there was handled at Port Los Angeles 32,415,615 pounds, or, say, 49.3 per cent of all, as against 13.3 per cent handled at San Pedro and East San Pedro and 37.4 per cent handled at Redondo.

This illustrates forcibly, I think, the value that the merchants place on Port Los Angeles, for they forward and receive via that port as much as they forward and receive by the way of San Pedro, East San Pedro, and Redondo.

The figures set forth in this letter can be relied upon, as they are gathered from the waybills of each road operating between Los Angeles and the ports named. Of course there is additional freight, which comes down by steamer for the interior, but that is a small amount comparatively, and cuts but little figure in the total tonnage.

My object is to show you the value that the merchants even now place on Port Los Angeles as against the other ports, both in the saving of time and proper facilities for handling.

I refer to what you probably know, i. e., that the large steamers of the Pacific Coast Steamship Company, like the *Corona* and *Santa Rosa,* stop only at Port Los Angeles and Redondo, while the small steamers only, like the *Eureka* and *Bonita,* stop at East San Pedro and San Pedro.

Yours, truly,

JNO. M. CRAWLEY.

Mr. WM. HOOD (care Nadeau Hotel, City).

EXHIBIT NO. 7.

OFFICE GENERAL FREIGHT AGENT.

SAN FRANCISCO, CAL., *December 5, 1896.*

DEAR SIR: In compliance with your memorandum of the 25th ultimo, calling for deep-sea tonnage, with names of deep-sea vessels, and local tonnage shown separately, passing Port Los Angeles, compared with San Pedro, for last twelve months, estimating tonnage handled by terminal road, inclosed please find original, with five additional copies each, as follows:

(1) Tonnage passing Port Los Angeles July 1, 1895, to June 30, 1896, inclusive, discharged from deep-sea vessels, from local coast vessels; delivered to deep-sea vessels, local coast vessels; names of deep-sea vessels; number of vessels landing deep-sea, local coast, lumber. (Figures used in this statement as to tonnage received and delivered from deep-sea craft obtained from agent, Port Los Angeles; other tonnage obtained from records furnished by freight auditor.)

(2) Tonnage passing San Pedro (inner harbor) July 1, 1895, to June 30, 1896, inclusive, discharged from local coast vessels; delivered to local coast vessels; showing tonnage carried by Southern Pacific Company and Terminal Railway. Some of the lumber was carried jointly by Terminal Railway and Southern California Railway. We are unable to segregate, as between these two carriers, the quantity carried by both; number of deep-sea carriers, the quantity carried by each. Have therefore shown lump sum carried by both; number of

126

DEEP-WATER HARBOR.

vessels landing, local coast and lumber. (Figures used here furnished by A. G. F. A. Crawley from data taken from records of the station.)

(3) Port Los Angeles versus San Pedro (inner harbor) July 1, 1895, to June 30, 1896, inclusive, compared. (Figures here used obtained from same source as shown above, Nos. 1 and 2.)

(4) Tonnage passing Port Los Angeles by commodities July 1, 1895, to June 30 1896, inclusive. (Figures here used furnished by freight auditor.)

(5) Merchandise, except lumber, passing San Pedro July 1, 1895, to June 30, 1896, inclusive, showing date calling, number of vessels, tons received or discharged. (This data furnished by A. G. F. A. Crawley, taken from the records of San Pedro station.)

(6) Lumber passing San Pedro (inner harbor) July 1, 1895, to June 30, 1896, showing date of calling, names of vessels, tons discharged or received. (These figures, also furnished by A. G. F. and P. A. Crawley, taken from station records.)

Have used the period ending June 30, 1896, because this is as late as we can get the data for within the time prescribed.

During this period there was no tonnage discharged from or delivered to vessels at San Pedro outer harbor.

Yours, truly,

C. F. SMURR.

Mr. J. C. STUBBS,
Third Vice-President, Southern Pacific Company Building.

Merchandise, except lumber, passing San Pedro (inner harbor) July 1, 1895, to June 30, 1896, inclusive.

DISCHARGED FROM COAST VESSELS.

Date	Vessel	Tons
1895.		
July 2	Steamer St. Paul	138
6	Steamer Eureka	42
10	Steamer St. Paul	84
14	Steamer Santa Cruz	45
17	Steamer Santa Cruz	58
18	Steamer St. Paul	33
22	Steamer Eureka	31
23	Steamer Eureka	56
30	Steamer St. Paul	21
Aug. 3	Steamer Eureka	17
7	Steamer Eureka	64
11	Steamer St. Paul	39
15	Steamer Eureka	43
19	Steamer St. Paul	85
23	Steamer St. Paul	30
27	Steamer Eureka	38
31	Steamer Eureka	46
Sept. 4	Steamer St. Paul	34
8	Steamer Eureka	32
12	Steamer St. Paul	47
16	Steamer Eureka	32
18	Schooner Penelope	5
20	Steamer Coos Bay	34
22	Steamer Eureka	46
25	Schooner Serena Thayer	216
26	Schooner Vina	288
28	Steamer St. Paul	73
Oct. 2	Steamer Eureka	83
6	Steamer St. Paul	168
10	Steamer St. Paul	128
15	Steamer Bonita	130
17	Schooner Norma	239
26	Steamer Eureka	630
28	Steamer Santa Cruz	24
30	Steamer St. Paul	322
Nov. 1	Steamer Santa Cruz	135
3	Steamer St. Paul	119
5	Steamer Eureka	49
7	Bark Ferris S. Thompson	82
11	Steamer St. Paul	40
15	Steamer St. Paul	44
18	Steamer Santa Cruz	48
19	Steamer Eureka	100

DEEP-WATER HARBOR.

Merchandise, except lumber, passing San Pedro (inner harbor) July 1, 1895, etc.—Cont'd.

DISCHARGED FROM COAST VESSELS—Continued.

Date	Vessel	Tons	Date	Vessel	Tons
1896.			**1896.**		
Apr. 27	Steamer Bonita	13	June 2	Steamer St. Paul	28
May 1	Steamer St. Paul	128	4	Steamer Bonita	49
3	Steamer Eureka	63	6	Steamer Eureka	61
9	Steamer St. Paul	129	10	Steamer St. Paul	37
13	Steamer Eureka	55	15	Steamer Eureka	39
18	Schooner Penelope	6	15	Steamer St. Paul	71
15	Steamer Santa Cruz	5	22	Steamer Eureka	60
17	Steamer St. Paul	67	27	Steamer St. Paul	54
21	Steamer Eureka	58		Total	9,162
25	Steamer St. Paul	27			
29	Steamer Eureka	15			

DELIVERED TO LOCAL COAST VESSELS.

Date	Vessel	Tons		Date	Vessel	Tons
1895.						
July 2	Steamer St. Paul	77		Steamer Eureka	77	
6	Steamer Eureka	37		Steamer St. Paul	17	
11	Steamer St. Paul	6		Steamer Eureka	5	
15	Steamer St. Paul	8		Steamer Eureka	6	
19	Steamer St. Paul	10		Steamer Eureka	10	
22	Steamer St. Paul	6		Schooner Annie		
27	Steamer St. Paul	7		Steamer St. Paul	101	
31	Steamer Eureka	7		Steamer St. Paul	70	
Aug. 4	Steamer Eureka	8		Steamer Eureka	23	
8	Steamer Eureka	12		Steamer St. Paul	198	
12	Steamer Eureka	35		Steamer Eureka	68	
16	Steamer Eureka	23		do.	95	
20	Steamer Eureka	4		Steamer St. Paul	7	
24	Steamer Eureka	13		Steamer St. Paul	1,125	
Sept. 5	Steamer St. Paul	50		Bark Enoch Talbot	2	
9	Steamer Eureka	10		Steamer St. Paul	230	
13	Steamer Eureka	3		Steamer Pasadena	52	
17	Steamer Eureka	19		Steamer St. Paul	4	
21	Steamer Eureka	28		Steamer Eureka	188	
25	Steamer Eureka	22		do.	11	
31	Steamer St. Paul	19		Steamer Annie	2	
Oct. 3	Steamer St. Paul	18		do.	105	
7	Steamer Eureka	42		Steamer St. Paul	10	
11	Steamer St. Paul	16		Steamer Eureka	96	
15	Steamer Eureka	19		Steamer St. Paul	5	
19	Steamer St. Paul	204		Steamer Eureka	130	
23	Steamer St. Paul	59		Steamer Eureka	111	
31	do.	35		Steamer Eureka	113	
Nov. 27	Steamer St. Paul	35		Steamer St. Paul	466	
	Steamer Eureka	13		Steamer Eureka	110	
12	Steamer St. Paul	6		Steamer Eureka	194	
18	Steamer Eureka	3		Steamer St. Paul	2	
24	Steamer Eureka	105		Steamer Eureka	19	
28	Steamer Eureka	1		Steamer St. Paul	10	
Dec. 2	Steamer St. Paul	21		Steamer Eureka	39	
6	do.	35		Steamer St. Paul	20	
10	Steamer Annie	9		Steamer Eureka	4	
14	Steamer Eureka	82		Steamer St. Paul	39	
18	Steamer St. Paul	7		do.	30	
22	Steamer Eureka	22		Steamer Eureka	30	
26	Steamer Eureka	58		Steamer Eureka	5	
30	Steamer Eureka	4		Steamer Eureka	6	
1896.				Steamer Eureka	5	
Jan. 3	Steamer St. Paul			Steamer St. Paul	12	
				Total	4,951	

RECAPITULATION.

Discharged from coast vessels	9,162
Delivered to local coast vessels	4,951
Total	14,113
Handled by—	
Southern Pacific Company	10,264
Los Angeles Terminal Company	3,849
Total	14,113

DEEP-WATER HARBOR.

Lumber passing San Pedro (inner harbor), July 1, 1895, to June 30, 1896.

DISCHARGED FROM COAST LUMBER CRAFT.

Date.	Vessel.	Tons.	Date.	Vessel.	Tons.
1895.			1895.		
July 1	Brig Courtney Ford	733	Sept. 22	Schooner Peerless	533
1	Schooner Lucy Ford	608	23	Schooner Mabel Gray	875
3	Schooner C. A. Holmes	1,000	23	Schooner J. M. Coleman	942
3	Schooner Barbara Hemster	291	25	Bark Tidal Wave	1,042
3	Bark Tidal Wave	1,541	25	Schooner Prosper	233
4	Schooner Prosper	959	26	Schooner Vina	225
4	Schooner Bangor	544	28	Schooner Pasadena	458
4	Schooner Peerless	450	28	Steamer Jewel	550
7	Schooner J. E. Leeds	450	Oct. 3	Steamer Lucy	602
10	Barkentine Skagit	602	3	Steamer Pasadena	716
14	Steamer Pasadena	716	5	Schooner Excelsior	833
14	Schooner Bertha Dolbeer	475	7	Schooner Kellogg	583
14	Steamer Tillamook	467	7	Steamer Louise	467
15	Schooner Alice	457	8	Schooner Muid of Orleans	383
18	Steamer Newsboy	88	8	Barkentine Planter	1,033
18	Schooner Newark	275	9	Schooner Comet	833
19	Schooner Una	472	12	Steamer Pasadena	500
19	Schooner C. E. Falk	648	12	Steamer Tillamook	481
19	Schooner Jessie Minor	625	4	Schooner Antelope	270
19	Schooner General Banning	400	6	Schooner San Buenaventura	403
23	Steamer Westport	487	24	Schooner Annie	358
25	Schooner Excelsior	733	25	Schooner Skagit	291
26	Schooner Letitia	417	26	Schooner Excelsior	1,083
27	Schooner Serena Thayer	458	27	Schooner W. F. Jewett	458
28	Steamer Viking	416	17	Schooner Monterey	291
28	Steamer Tillamook	497	17	Schooner Jessie Minor	497
28	Steamer National City	553	17	Steamer Tillamook	467
28	Steamer Pasadena	450	23	Schooner Jewel	550
30	Schooner Barbara Hemster	283	23	Schooner Alice	283
Aug. 1	Schooner Louisa	700	23	Schooner Reporter	700
2	Schooner Comet	833	23	Schooner Salvator	833
3	Schooner Tallant	1,300	29	Schooner El Norah	643
6	Barkentine Monitor	643	30	Schooner Holmes	500
9	Schooner Jewel	500	31	Schooner Lillie Bonne	834
9	Steamer J. W. Weatherwax	834	31	Barkentine Monitor	521
11	Barkentine Monitor	466	31	Steamer Mabel Gray	388
11	Schooner Gironde	450	31	Steamer Marie Smith	750
11	Steamer Reporter	732	Nov. 3	Steamer Bartlett	1,033
11	Schooner Lizzie Vance	858	3	Barkentine J. M. Griffith	683
	Steamer Protection	333	3	Schooner Louise	83
	Steamer National City	83	7	Schooner Excelsior	681
	Barkentine Uncle John	760	7	Steamer Serena Thayer	1,133
	Schooner Redfield	550	11	Steamer Bangor	250
	Steamer Excelsior	496	11	Steamer Protection	1,000
	Schooner E. Norah	417	11	Steamer Jewel	417
14	Schooner Allen A	708	12	Steamer Protection	708
13	Schooner Glendale	592	12	Steamer Pasadena	450
13	Schooner Lucy	633	12	Steamer Meteor	500
13	Schooner Sadie	133	13	Schooner Meteor	612
18	Steamer Caspar	900	13	Schooner Ethel Zoane	525
22	Steamer Caspar	433	13	Brig Tanner	1,000
28	Steamer National City	333	13	Brig Courtney Ford	877
28	Schooner M. C. Rose	558	13	Schooner S. C. Holmes	1,167
28	Steamer Pasadena	458	21	Schooner Halcyon	833
29	Schooner Alice	450	22	Schooner Alcatraz	522
31	Schooner Westport	475	22	Barkentine Clikifat	1,075
Sept. 1	Schooner C. S. Holmes	1,000	23	Steamer Alcatraz	545
1	Schooner Newark	66	23	Steamer G. W. Watson	670
5	Barkentine J. M. Griffith	1,100	24	Steamer Lucie	992
5	Barkentine Skagit	1,028	24	Steamer Ivy	608
6	Schooner Nokomis	1,217	26	Schooner Pasadena	333
6	Steamer Jewel	1,505	26	Schooner J. M. Coleman	392
6	Brig Tanner	488	29	Steamer Jewel	958
10	Steamer Pasadena	458	30	Steamer Alcatraz	542
10	Steamer Alcatraz	604	Dec. 5	Bark Tidal Wave	1,000
13	Schooner Witzman	912	5	Steamer Protection	611
13	Schooner C. E. Falk	686	6	Schooner Norma	666
15	Schooner Ina	488	6	Steamer Tillamook	750
16	Steamer Newsboy	225	9	Steamer Excelsior	66
16	Steamer Annie	583	10	Steamer Pasadena	448
16	Schooner Louise	353	10	Steamer Prosper	500
17	Steamer Tillamook	716	17	Steamer Tillamook	1,397
18	Schooner Meteor	475	18	Steamer Meteor	292
18	Schooner Barbara Hemster	400	18	Schooner Barbara Hemster	1,050
18	Brig Geneva	1,266	13	Brig Enoch Talbot	50
22	Schooner Prosper	1,492	13	Schooner Alcatraz	292
22	Schooner Alcatraz	42	15	Schooner Comet	517
22	Schooner Ruby A. Cousins	383			

DEEP-WATER HARBOR.

Lumber passing San Pedro (inner harbor), July 1, 1895, to June 30, 1896—Continued.

DISCHARGED FROM COAST LUMBER CRAFT—Continued.

Date.	Vessel.	Tons.	Date.	Vessel.	Tons.
1895.					
Dec. 16	Schooner H. C. Wright	666		Schooner Dora Blenner	666
16	Steamer Queen	558		Steamer Lakme	833
16	Schooner Alice	450	Mar. 14	Schooner El Norah	450
16	Schooner Birdie Minor	533	15	Schooner Sadie	625
18	Schooner J. M. Coleman	1,083	15	Steamer National City	583
23	Bark Retriever	643	18	Schooner Peerless	538
25	Bark Monitor	766	23	Steamer Pasadena	500
25	Steamer Lakme	450	25	Steamer Tillamook	521
25	Schooner Serena Thayer	786	25	Steamer Navarro	521
26	Schooner Annie Larsen	933	26	Schooner Meteor	286
25	Steamer Excelsior	500	26	Steamer Bangor	1,266
25	Steamer Lucy	464	28	Schooner C. A. Thayer	1,000
25	Steamer Tillamook	700	28	Schooner Louise	950
30	Schooner Louise	575	30	Schooner Sadie	671
30	Bark Katie Flickenger	966	31	Schooner E. Weller	673
27	Schooner Salvator	916	31	Schooner Comet	766
28	Schooner S. C. Holmes	1,000	Apr. 6	Schooner Mary E. Ross	1,000
28	Schooner Reporter	708	7	Schooner Corona	416
28	Schooner Premier	700	7	Schooner C. S. Holmes	883
1896.			7	Steamer National City	958
Jan. 6	Schooner Bartlett	1,017	13	Schooner Serena Thayer	363
8	Schooner Lottie Carson	542	13	Schooner J. M. Weatherwax	493
8	Schooner El Norah	464	13	Steamer Alcatraz	492
8	Schooner Pasadena	512	16	Ollie Ford	833
10	Steamer Excelsior	296	19	Barkentine Monitor	533
11	Steamer Tillamook	471	20	Steamer Pasadena	508
13	Steamer Lakme	1,000	20	Schooner Alice	411
13	Steamer National City	533	22	Steamer Jewel	500
14	Steamer Annie Larsen	1,083	22	Schooner Una	500
22	Steamer Jewel	1,275	28	Schooner Sadie	733
22	Schooner Meteor	583	28	Steamer El Norah	450
22	Steamer Lucy	500	May 29	Schooner Occidental	612
23	Steamer Pasadena	916		Schooner Azalea	245
23	Steamer Bangor	200		Schooner C. E. Falk	298
23	Bark Ferris S. Thompson	591	3	Steamer Jewel	400
24	Schooner Vesta	83	3	Steamer Alcazar	750
24	Brig Tanner	467	14	Steamer Pasadena	650
24	Steamer Navarro	1,050	14	Steamer Tillamook	508
26	Schooner Edw. Parke	238	16	Steamer Lakme	500
26	Schooner Ethel Zahne	507	17	Schooner Peerless	666
29	Steamer Excelsior	537	June 29	Steamer Jewel	600
29	Schooner Lizzie Bonner	583		Steamer Jewell Dolbeer	600
29	Schooner Jessie Minor	450		Schooner Bertha Dolbeer	450
Feb. 3	Schooner Alice	480	24	Schooner Bonita	450
3	Steamer Sadie	538	30	Steamer Monterey	480
3	Schooner El Norah	533	31	Steamer Pasadena	483
7	Schooner Alice	287	31	Schooner S. C. Holmes	283
7	Steamer Serena Thayer	648	31	Schooner Alice	500
7	Steamer Comet	700	4	Steamer Comet	931
7	Schooner Alcalde	666	4	Schooner Redfield	1,320
10	Steamer Pasadena	500	5	Steamer National City	450
10	Schooner Beulah	500	8	Steamer Mary Buhne	833
10	Brig Courtney Ford	833	10	Schooner Bangor	1,000
14	Schooner S. C. Holmes	933	10	Steamer Fanny Adele	27
14	Steamer Excelsior	550	12	Steamer Ray Sommers	283
18	Schooner Halcyon	540	13	Steamer Tillamook	916
19	Brigantine Portland	1,000	13	Steamer National City	503
19	Steamer Sunol	610	15	Schooner Pasadena	583
19	Steamer Caspar	322	22	Schooner Lakme	500
25	Steamer Pasadena	500	25	Barkentine Uncle John	1,050
25	Steamer National City	466	28	Steamer Alcazar	666
29	Schooner Tillamook	503	28	Steamer Pasadena	158
29	Schooner Salvator	666		Steamer Pasadena	500
Mar. 3	Schooner Reporter	223			
3	Steamer Caspar	666		**Total**	**184,809**
4	Schooner S. C. Falck	667			
4	Schooner Alcazar	611			
11	Steamer Pasadena	600			
11	Schooner Jessie Minor	466			
14	Schooner Alice	666			

DELIVERED TO COAST LUMBER CRAFT.

Date.	Vessel.	Tons.	Date.	Vessel.	Tons.
1895.			1896.		
Dec. 7	Steamer Protection	375	Jan. 12	Steamer Excelsior	385
19	Steamer Lakme	383	Feb. 27	Steamer National City	283
29	Steamer Excelsior	66		**Total**	**1,400**

DEEP-WATER HARBOR.

RECAPITULATION.

Coast lumber craft:

	Tons.
Discharged from	184,809
Delivered to	1,490
Total	186,299

Handled by—

	Tons.
Southern Pacific Company	137,391
Los Angeles Terminal Company	48,908
Total	186,299

PORT LOS ANGELES V. SAN PEDRO (INNER HARBOR).

Tonnage handled during period July 1, 1895, to June 30, 1896, inclusive.

Port Los Angeles	Tons.	Tons.	San Pedro	Tons.	Tons.
Discharged from—			Discharged from—		
Deep-sea vessels—			Deep-sea vessels	9,162	184,809
Cement	11,923		Local coast vessels—		
Coal	13,122		Merchandise		
Coke	309		Lumber		
Merchandise	7,677				193,971
		33,031			
Local coast vessels—			Delivered to—		
Cement	809		Deep-sea vessels		
Coal	115,254		Local coast vessels—		
Coke	42		Lumber	1,490	
Merchandise	15,965		Merchandise	4,951	
Lumber	28,325		Total		6,441
		160,395	Total		200,412
Delivered to—					
Deep-sea vessels—					
Grain	2,240				
Local coast vessels—					
Grain	1,537				
Merchandise	5,201				
		8,978			
Total		202,404			

Merchandise at San Pedro:

	Tons.
Southern Pacific Company carried	10,264
Los Angeles Terminal Railway carried	3,849

Lumber at San Pedro:

	Tons.
Southern Pacific Company carried	137,391
Los Angeles Terminal Railway and Southern California Railway carried	48,908

Names of deep-sea vessels discharged or loaded at Port Los Angeles.—Ships: Eclipse, Fingal, Lady Isabella, Eaton Hall, Port Elgin, Airlie, St. John, Dunboyne, Philadelphia, Chas. E. Moody, Dunsyre. Barks: Edinburghshire, Forfarshire, Fernbank.

Number of calls made.

	Port Los Angeles.	San Pedro.
Deep-sea vessels	14	0
Local coast vessels	156	116
Lumber craft	69	298
Total	239	414

No tonnage handled at anchorage or outer harbor of San Pedro.

DEEP-WATER HARBOR.

Tonnage passing Port Los Angeles, from July 1, 1895, to June 30, 1896.

Discharged from vessels.	Tons.	Delivered to vessels.	Tons.
Merchandise	12,708	Merchandise	3,178
Grain	141	Grain	3,777
Flour	511	Mill stuffs	12
Mill stuffs	229	Fruit, dried	13
Fruit, green	20	Fruit, green	102
Vegetables	1,031	Honey	
Hops	10	Packing house products	15
Other agricultural products	969	Wool	4
Fish	11	Hides and skins	56
Wool	128,376	Asphaltum	1,309
Coal	351	Other mineral products	12
Coke	48	Iron, pig, etc	12
Bituminous rock	138	Cement	55
Clay	49	Beer, wine, etc	264
Stone	553	Petroleum, etc	49
Salt	42	Lumber	84
Other mineral products	1,056		36
Iron, pig, etc	144		
Cement	12,732		
Brick	290		
Beer, wine, etc	2,235		
Sugar	2,712		
Petroleum, etc	516		
Other manufactures	28,325		
Lumber	166		
Miscellaneous			
Total	193,426	Total	8,978

	Tons.
Total discharged	193,426
Total delivered	8,978
Grand total	202,404

Distances from Arcade Depot, Los Angeles.

	Miles.
Santa Monica	17.2
Port Los Angeles	20.4
End of Port Los Angeles Wharf, station 170 + 22.9	20.4
San Pedro	21.8
End of proposed San Pedro Wharf, station 170	25
Declez	48.97
Declez Quarry (+ 1.77)	50.74
Chatsworth Park	32.9
Declez, to end of Port Los Angeles Wharf	69.37
Declez Quarry to end of Port Los Angeles Wharf	71.14
Declez Quarry to end of proposed San Pedro Wharf	75.74
Chatsworth Park to end of proposed San Pedro Wharf	57.9
Chatsworth Park to end of Port Los Angeles Wharf	53.3

PORT LOS ANGELES, CAL., *May 7, 1896.*

EDITOR NEW YORK MARITIME REGISTER:

I have finished discharging a cargo of 2,800 long tons of general cargo, from New York, at Port Los Angeles and taken on board 550 tons of ballast, and can say that the work done here in discharging ships, both for speed and carefulness of handling, can not be surpassed anywhere.

The Southern Pacific Company does everything in their power to assist the shipping, and shipowners sending their vessels here will find their interests are looked out after.

I consider Port Los Angeles a safe port, and would be glad to accept another charter for there at any time.

Yours, respectfully,

R. L. LEONARD,
Master American ship Chas. E. Moody.

DEEP-WATER HARBOR.

SALT LAKE CITY, *December 18, 1896.*

Admiral JOHN G. WALKER, U. S. N.
Chairman of Commission to Locate Deep-Water Harbor, Los Angeles, Cal.:

The Salt Lake Chamber of Commerce, at a meeting held this day, unanimously resolved to present to your Commission, on behalf of said city and the State of Utah, the fact that this State is deeply interested in the proper location of the proposed deep-water harbor for southern California, for the reason that our citizens are engaged in an effort to build a line of railroad to connect this city with Los Angeles and the proposed harbor. This railroad when completed will be the shortest line between the Atlantic and Pacific oceans. In southern Utah, along the proposed line, and not more than 500 miles from tide water, occur vast deposits of iron ore fully equal in extent and quality to the great iron ranges of Michigan. Contiguous to these great iron deposits there exists coal measures of almost unlimited extent. Considering the future growth and development of the Pacific Coast, and contemplating the scarcity of coal and iron on the Pacific merce of that region, and of South America, Australasia, and the Orient, we deem it of the utmost importance that a suitable harbor be secured near Los Angeles by which these invaluable products of our State may reach this great and growing market. The arrangements are well advanced to commence the construction of this railroad.

We expect to cooperate in the building of this line with the Los Angeles Terminal Company, and we are fully convinced that the construction of the road will be materially advanced, and, in fact, rendered certain, by the location of this deep-water harbor at San Pedro.

The chamber is so earnest that no mistake be made in the selection of the site most advantageous to this State, that it has appointed the Hon. Charles O. Whitemore to appear before your Commission and present these resolutions and to personally urge the many advantages which we think will accrue to Utah, Nevada, California, and the nation by the selection of San Pedro as the deep-water harbor for southern California.

SALT LAKE CHAMBER OF COMMERCE.
By W. A. NELDEN, *President.*

Attest:
[SEAL.]

EDWARD T. COLBORN, *Secretary.*

I appear before the Board as the representative of the Los Angeles Terminal Railway Company, a corporation with which I have been connected, either in the capacity of vice-president or attorney, since its organization.

The corporation was organized for the purpose of acquiring, owning, and leasing to larger systems of railway terminal facilities in the city of Los Angeles and upon the ocean at San Pedro Harbor. It has already spent some three millions of dollars in purchasing land and making improvements with this end in view.

It may be unnecessary to say that I shall not endeavor to touch upon any of the technical features involved in the selection of a proper site for the proposed harbor, but shall confine myself in what I shall have to say, with reference to the respective harbor locations named in the law under which your Board was appointed, to the merits or demerits of the proposed places as they may affect companies engaged in land transportation, and I shall endeavor to call your attention to those points in each location which, from a somewhat careful study of the respective locations, appear to me to be most favorable or unfavorable to the operation as successful and efficient servants of commerce at each place of transportation agencies of the kind that I represent.

It may, however, be of some assistance to the Board in understanding the points which I shall endeavor to make if I am permitted to give a short history of the development in marine and land transportation agencies which have occurred within the last few years upon the coast contiguous to the city of Los Angeles.

In the year 1880 the city of Los Angeles was a comparatively small town, shown by the census to contain, I believe, 15,000 population. This population increased with something like ordinary growth until about 1885, when the building into the city of the Santa Fe Railway afforded that country a second transcontinental line— the Southern Pacific having been the first. This was immediately followed by what was known as the "boom" period, which produced such an immense increase in population and growth in development of the country that the census of 1890 showed Los Angeles to be a city of 50,000 people and to have experienced during the decade from 1880 to 1890 a growth of 351 per cent, being the maximum of municipal growth shown in the United States for that period. The boom brought with it a large growth of commercial interests, some idea of which may be gained from the testimony of Captain Welt as to the number of deep-water vessels that found anchorage at San

---

DEEP-WATER HARBOR.

Pedro during the years between 1884 and 1889, which were the years that marked the growth, culmination, and decadence of the boom. As the intense and somewhat unnatural business activity of the boom decreased, the number of vessels coming to San Pedro—at that time the only port for Los Angeles—also began to show a falling off, until by 1890 there was nothing like the amount of commerce to this part of the coast as there was during the period of the boom's existence. A considerable portion of that commerce had also been attracted to another and newer port. In the year 1887 a wealthy transportation company, which before that time had been operating on the northern Pacific Coast, purchased several hundred acres of land on the bay of Santa Monica at a place which has been referred to here as Redondo. They there erected a substantial pier, which, owing to the peculiar formation of the bottom of the ocean at that place bringing deep water close in to shore, was built at a very moderate cost. The company also constructed a line of railway from their pier to the city of Los Angeles. This pier was opened for business in the latter part of 1888, and during that year the Santa Fe Railroad also built a line connecting it with this city. I think that I may safely say that from the date that pier and the railways connecting it with Los Angeles were opened to traffic until the pier at Port Los Angeles was completed, the Redondo Pier accommodated, as a port of call, nearly all the deep-draft vessels coming to this part of the coast with consignment of general cargoes for Los Angeles, by reason of the fact that such vessels could there unload directly upon the cars without the expensive and troublesome method of lightering their cargoes to the shore followed at the San Pedro anchorage. The Redondo Pier had in addition become a regular port of call for the vessels engaged in the coast traffic between San Francisco and San Diego, and by reason of being somewhat nearer in point of time to the city of Los Angeles for the business from the direction of San Francisco it had from the first secured a large part of that traffic.

By the year 1890 the city of Los Angeles had become of such importance commercially, and the country tributary to it had increased so largely in population, that it became evident to its commercial interests that the future development of the city and surrounding country required, for the proper accommodation of its probable future maritime commerce, a harbor in the fullest sense of the term, and not a mere port of call such as had been and would be the character of the unprotected anchorage at San Pedro. This feeling was emphasized by the fact that Los Angeles was the only point on the coast having competing lines of transcontinental railways, and by the further fact that those lines of roads afforded a shorter land route for the commerce of the Pacific islands and the Orient to the cities of the East than did any of the other railways reaching the Pacific Coast, and were not exposed to interference by storms and winter snows such as for some months of the year seriously cripple other transcontinental railways.

Impelled by these considerations, the business community of the city of Los Angeles and the surrounding country began an earnest agitation for the construction of a deep-water harbor which should be capable of accommodating in the best manner the maritime commerce which they hoped their superior railway facilities would attract. The first substantial result of this effort was that in the river and harbor act approved September 19, 1890, provision was made for the appointment of a Board of Engineers to examine the Pacific Coast between Points Dume and Capistrano with a view of determining the best location for a deep-water harbor.

On December 18, 1891, the report of the Board was made selecting San Pedro as the best site for the proposed deep-water harbor, and that report is before this Board as Executive Document No. 39 of the Fifty-second Congress.

I may say, in passing, that during the consideration by the Board of the matters submitted to them, arguments were presented favoring the two places—San Pedro and Santa Monica—the Santa Monica arguments being presented under the auspices of an organization formed in that seaside town.

Influenced by the belief that a determination of the matter submitted to the harbor Board by the act of September 19, 1890, would result in the construction of such a deep-water harbor as was sought, and in confidence that the harbor would be constructed at San Pedro, a body of Eastern capitalists prepared to organize the Los Angeles Terminal Railway Company, and purchased in the latter part of the year 1890 certain properties in the city of Los Angeles and upon the water front from the inner harbor at San Pedro, for the purposes which I have heretofore mentioned. Beginning in the early part of the year 1891, this company during the year constructed a line of railway extending from the city of Los Angeles to its properties on the bay of San Pedro. It was also a part of its scheme to promote the building of a line of railway extending from Salt Lake City and forming a direct connection with its terminals in Los Angeles, and at the harbor, for the purpose of giving a direct connection with this coast to about 10,000 miles of railway lines having termini at Salt Lake City, and not then, or at present, having any direct connection with this coast. This would also have had the advantage of being by about 300 miles the shortest line between this point and Eastern cities.

About the middle of the year 1888, the same year that witnessed the opening for business of the Redondo Pier, the Southern Pacific Company discontinued the work upon its pier projected into the outer anchorage at San Pedro.

The deed records of our county show that on July 30, 1891, a deed was executed conveying from Abbott Kinney to Frank H. Davis—whom it is understood from the statements made before the Board is the representative of Mr. Huntington—certain property fronting for 2,200 feet on Santa Monica Bay, commonly known and described as the Santa Monica Heights tract.

On December 23, 1891, a deed was executed by John P. Jones and Arcadia Baker, conveying to the Southern Pacific Railroad Company the right of way for a railroad which that company now uses between its tunnel and its wharf at Port Los Angeles, excepting that portion running through the 2,200 feet of frontage of the Santa Monica Heights tract, which appears to have been conveyed by Frank H. Davis by deed dated December 28, 1891.

In the latter part of 1891, or the beginning of 1892, the Southern Pacific Company began the extension of its tracks from the terminus which it had theretofore had in the town of Santa Monica to the present site of its pier at Port Los Angeles, and began the construction of that pier.

In January of the year 1892 the commercial interests of the city of Los Angeles decided to make a strong effort to secure from Congress, then sitting, an appropriation to begin work upon the deep-water harbor as recommended by the Board of 1891. In this matter the company which I represent was, of course, deeply interested, and in January of that year Mr. Charles Forman, a citizen of means and myself, representing the Los Angeles Terminal Railway Company, went to Washington City for the purpose of appearing before the Senate Committee on Commerce and urging the propriety and necessity of that committee favorably recommending a measure which had been introduced by Senator Charles N. Felton, then representing this State in the Senate, appropriating about $250,000 to make the port of San Pedro the proposed harbor. Shortly after we reached Washington City a day was appointed by the Commerce Committee for the consideration of Mr. Felton's measure, and Mr. Forman and myself were to have had a hearing before the Commerce Committee for the purpose of urging a favorable report. When the matter was called up upon the day appointed, Senator Frye, chairman of the committee, exhibited to the committee a telegram which he had just received from the chief engineer of the Southern Pacific Company stating that the holding ground for ships in the area of the proposed deep-water harbor at San Pedro was bad, and suggesting the propriety of a further investigation upon that point when the Government undertook the large expenditure recommended by the Board of 1891 for the construction there of a deep-water harbor. This destroyed any chances for favorable recommendation which Senator Felton's measure might have had. In order that no time should be lost upon the matter, Senator Felton immediately took steps which resulted in the appointment of the Board of Engineers of 1892, Colonel Craighill chairman. The report of that Board, and the subsequent history of the question, is probably so well known to this Board that it is not necessary for me to touch upon it.

I trust that I may be pardoned, however, in observing that, in the light of the statements which have been made upon this hearing as to the equality of merit in the holding ground at the two places, it was probably unfortunate for the interests of commerce upon this coast that the question of the possible defective character of the holding ground at San Pedro should ever have been raised, and the fact that it was raised may to some extent account for the attitude which has been assumed toward this matter by certain Members of Congress, for it is a certain fact that this matter of holding ground has been of such effect in some quarters that Senator Frye, in the speech which he made upon this harbor question on May 11 and 12 last, in the Senate of the United States, speaking of a report which an engineer had made to Mr. Huntington as to the demerits of San Pedro, said: "He [the engineer] said that a large part of the area within the breakwater was upon rocky bottom and there was no proper holding ground. On this report [continued the Senator] the Southern Pacific Railroad deserted the $3,000,000 planted down at San Pedro and went up and planted $1,000,000 in building at Santa Monica * * * the finest wharf or pier in the whole world." And we find the statement reiterated in Mr. Huntington's letter to Secretary Lamont of date as late as June 16 of this year (see Document F, of the typewritten documents filed by Mr. Corthell with your Board).

The outgrowth of the whole matter, after the years in which it has been under discussion, has been the appointment of this Board whom I have the honor now to address.

I think it will be seen from the foregoing that the harbor sought by the commercial interests which had begun and have prosecuted this effort to obtain a deep-water harbor upon the portion of the coast near the city of Los Angeles, was a harbor offering advantages to commerce entirely different from and much more

S. Doc. 18——17

extensive than were offered by either of the then existing ports—San Pedro or Redondo—or any port of that character.

It was in anticipation of the construction upon this coast of such a harbor that the corporation which I represent invested its money here, and with the further anticipation that when such a harbor was constructed it would be of sufficient commercial importance to the large extent of country lying east of California to enable its promotors to offer such inducements as would secure for their terminal system a connection with the railway lines having their western termini at Salt Lake City, and for which the proposed harbor would be the nearest and best Pacific Coast port.

It may be pertinent here to quote to this Board what the Board of Engineers of 1892 said in their report as to the commercial significance of the proposed harbor. On page 4 of their report occurs the following:

"By far the most important aspect of this subject, however, is its relation to the probable future development of the deep-sea commerce of the country. Heretofore the Asiatic trade has naturally gone to San Francisco, but it has been pointed out that the construction of the Canadian and Northern Pacific railroads has introduced two competitors for the overland transportation of the Asiatic commerce. Two through lines, the Southern Pacific and the Santa Fe systems, cross the continent from Los Angeles at much lower elevations than the northern lines, and also connect the Pacific with the Gulf of Mexico, and their operation is never obstructed by snow or ice. If a safe, accessible, and convenient harbor for deep-draft vessels existed on the southern coast, these would appear the most favorable lines for the transportation of Asiatic and Australian commerce.

"Should the Nicaragua Canal be completed, the importance of the proposed harbor will become still greater. At the present time the most convenient course for sailing vessels coming around the Horn is to go out in the mid-Pacific and strike the trade winds to make the port of San Francisco. With the completion of the canal commerce will be principally transported by steam vessels of moderate draft, which will move north along the coast and seek the nearest favorable and convenient port from which their freight can reach its market.

"A deep-water harbor on the southern coast would thus receive the Asiatic and Australian freights for shipment over the most favorable transcontinental lines, accommodate a large part of the commerce passing through the Nicaragua Canal which now goes around the Horn, and finally furnish a port of shipment and supply, not only for the productive territory in its immediate vicinity, but also for the great interior plateau reached by the southern railways beyond the mountain ranges. Considering, therefore, the probable needs of commerce in the near future, the Board is of the opinion that the proposed deep-water harbor is of high national importance and well worthy of construction by the General Government."

If the provision of this Board expressed in the foregoing quotation shall be realized—and there would seem to be no reason why it may not be, and many reasons why it probably will be—the harbor which this Board is now called upon to locate will probably, at no distant date, become the most important harbor upon the Pacific Coast, commanding, as it will, the major part of the transcontinental commerce and being the first to receive for distribution over the western half of the continent the great commerce which certainly will come from the East through the Nicaragua Canal when it is completed.

In such a harbor I submit it is of paramount importance that the facilities for its use by competing lines of transportation and by all commercial interests which may desire to have access to its waters for the purpose of receiving or shipping freight should be the most extensive, convenient, and inexpensive possible. These prime necessities will, in my opinion, be impossible of attainment at the harbor which the Southern Pacific Company proposes shall be constructed by the Government in Santa Monica Bay, for the reason that there can be no competitive use, in a broad commercial sense, of that harbor.

This Board, from personal observation, is aware that the coast line facing the whole of the protected area of the harbor at that place consists of cliffs averaging about 175 feet in height, separated from the water by a very narrow strip of sandy beach in width at some places a little more than 100 feet; that for a distance of over 2 miles the only approach to the area protected by the proposed breakwater is also a narrow beach; that the Southern Pacific Company is the owner of a considerable portion of the width of this approach for all of the distance and of nearly the full width where its 100 feet width of right of way begins at the eastern edge of the protected area of the harbor. That portion of the proposed water front not owned by the Southern Pacific is shown by the map filed with this Board by Mr. Hawgood to be owned by Messrs. Jones and Baker. We have thus a proposed location for a harbor which the Government is asked to construct whose whole water front and the narrow approaches thereto are entirely owned by three proprietors.

It is true that the act authorizing the existence of this Board provides that before the money appropriated to be expended, the Southern Pacific Company shall execute an agreement to share equally with any other railroad company paying its proportion of the cost "the use of its pier and the approaches thereto situated westerly of the easterly entrance of the Santa Monica Tunnel."

It will be observed, however, that the provisions of the law do not extend to sharing or dividing with any company any property which it may have obtained on this water front other than that used for approaches to its present existing pier and the pier itself. It will also be observed from the maps filed with this Board by the Southern Pacific engineers that this company owns a strip of land aligning the water front of that half of the protected area of the proposed harbor extending westward and beyond its present pier. To this holding, and to any piers which may be constructed in the west half of the harbor and to which this land might be used as an approach, it would appear that this law will not apply.

It has also appeared in evidence that a person deeply interested in the welfare of the Southern Pacific Company owns in fee the land fronting the proposed harbor for 2,200 feet, extending eastward from the present pier of the Southern Pacific, which is situated exactly in the center of the proposed protected area. The ownership of this land carries with it, under the laws of this State, title in fee to mean high tide. An examination of the map which I herewith file with this Board will show that between the line of mean high tide and the southerly or ocean line of the 100-foot strip of right of way which the Southern Pacific Company has acquired through this property, there is a small line of beach constituting a sufficient holding to entitle the owner to invoke the right of accretion in asserting a sufficient holding to entitle the owner to use this land as landing places for other wharves, and those wharves and the approaches thereto over this land strip of land will not be subject to the requirement of the law as to joint ownership. It is probable that for the remaining 2,000 feet next to the eastern line of the proposed protected area of this harbor the protection would not be sufficient to encourage the building of long and costly wharves in that portion. Certainly wharves located there would not be so favorably situated for the transaction of business as would be those located on the other and more protected portions of the harbor.

So, we have in this harbor a railroad company already occupying a right of way along the whole 8,000 feet of the proposed front, only half of which is subject to the law with reference to joint ownership, but all of which forms approaches to wharves which may be run out into any portion of the protected area from any part of the frontage. In addition to that, this company practically controls all of the available land for other purposes on 2,200 feet of the 4,400 feet of water front which will enjoy the maximum of protection, and such control, outside the narrow right of way from the tunnel to the present pier, is not subject to the provision as to joint ownership. Should the commerce of this port increase to an extent which will make the building of other wharves necessary under the conditions as they exist, it is not hard to imagine the occupancy by the Southern Pacific Company of practically all of the protected area by wharves which it shall construct, only one of which, and the narrow approaches thereto, would be subject to the provisions as to joint ownership and control. So that it is not going beyond the bare facts of the case to say that along the whole front of this harbor the Southern Pacific has, and will have, in spite of the provisions of this law, a superior right which no other company can afford, or will endeavor to compete with. It is unnecessary for me to call the attention of the Board to the intolerable burdens which, by virtue of this ownership of property along the whole of the front, a large portion of which is not affected by the law as to joint ownership and use, might, and certainly would, be imposed by this company on any rival company attempting to compete with it for the business of this harbor.

It has been said that a railroad company could avail itself of the right of eminent domain for the purpose of condemning over the land not owned by the Southern Pacific an entrance into this harbor. But, under the conditions which surround it, before anything like a fair competitive line of the harbor can be secured by other transportation interests, it will, I apprehend, be necessary to work a change in the sort of human nature which usually dominates and controls competing business enterprises.

It is a serious question, too, whether, under the provisions of the law, the joint right of use provided for over the present approach of the Southern Pacific to its wharf could be used by any company which might desire to go beyond that wharf and build a wharf of its own, inasmuch as the law only provides for the equal sharing of "the pier now constructed on the site of said harbor and the approaches thereto." In the absence of such a right, and upon the failure of the Southern Pacific Company to fully occupy the protected area for wharves extending out from the right of way, it might be possible for a competing railroad company to, at large expense, acquire, by condemnation, a very narrow right of way along the entire narrow approach to the harbor, and also through the land of Mr. Huntington, and so run a line into the

harbor front to a point where it could put a wharf out in the area of the protected harbor. But such condition of [affairs] prohibits the construction and ownership of wharves by individuals, or by an [organization] not endowed with the power of eminent domain for condemning land.

It is true that under the laws of California an individual or a company having [obtained] a franchise to construct and maintain a wharf can condemn a land appro[ach] to such wharf of sufficient dimensions to form a landing place for the wharf on the shore. But such individual or company has no power to condemn a highway for an outlet to the business of such wharf, and at the harbor in question it would be necessary for every person or corporation desiring to construct and use a wharf extending from that portion of the water front controlled by Mr. Huntington to secure in some way a control of the land lying between it and the railway right of way subject to joint use. It is difficult to see how this could be done, as the ownership of a franchise to construct and maintain a wharf conveys with it no power to condemn a way leading from it to any other point. I apprehend, however, that should the harbor be constructed at Santa Monica there would be no attempt at private ownership to wharves.

I am not advised as to the exact expenditures which the Southern Pacific found necessary in order to reach a practical depth of water at that point; but in his letter to Secretary Lamont—a copy of which is Document F of the typewritten documents filed by Mr. Corthell with this Board—Mr. Huntington, the president of that company, says: "We went to Port Los Angeles and built a great pier there which cost us, I think, about $1,000,000."

I also notice that in the speech upon the merits of the proposed harbors, which I have referred to above, Senator Frye states that "the Southern Pacific planted $1,000,000 in building at Santa Monica * * *" the finest wharf or pier in the whole world." But however much or little the wharf may have cost, it is hardly probable that with the difficulties which might be interposed by the company now holding the superior right along the whole of that harbor in view, any private party or company will be induced to expend the very large amount of money necessary to build a wharf of over 4,000 feet long required to reach deep water at that point.

In addition to the foregoing a most serious aspect of the case is the burden upon commerce which will be entailed by the necessity of obtaining a fair return upon the investment from the commerce passing over wharves costing in the first instance so much to build, and in the second instance so much to maintain against the destructive insects which frequent the warm waters of the Pacific Coast. And it is not possible at that place to accommodate any sort of commerce, even the comparatively light-draft coasting lumber vessels, in any other way than upon a long and expensive wharf.

These conditions, I submit, are such as to make any railway company desiring to reach upon this coast a harbor which shall attract an extensive foreign and domestic commerce despair of accomplishing that end at Port, Los Angeles, for the reason that it seems improbable that, under existing conditions, any commerce will be attracted to that port, save such as can be secured by the company which has already the superior rights there. And it appears quite certain that what commerce may be induced to come there will be controlled by the Southern Pacific Company through the special privileges and concessions which that company will be enabled to offer it, and which no other company can hope to equal.

Taking the Southern Pacific statement as to the cost of its own wharf, it is not going out of the way to say that the first cost of wharves necessary to be constructed in that harbor within the next ten years, should anything like a considerable business be developed there, will equal the cost of constructing the harbor itself, and this counts nothing for the enormous cost of maintaining such structures in the waters of this latitude.

But it is, I submit, not to be imagined that any considerable commerce can be enjoyed by a harbor offering no opportunities in the way of the construction of warehouses for the accommodation of such freights as can not be economically handled from the ship to the cars, and vice versa, or for affording vessels such accommodations as they may require beyond the mere furnishing to them of a place to discharge their cargoes on to cars. It is not conceivable that any harbor that has, and can have, no provisions for docking, cleaning, and repairing ships can ever be more than a mere port of call.

Persons familiar with the harbor of San Francisco know that frequently vessels come to that port over the long distances from the ports of the Pacific islands and the Orient buffeted and battered by the storms which they encounter, for whose accommodation such interior basins and docks are absolutely a necessity. It is impossible to see how such things could be afforded at the proposed harbor, and in their absence it will certainly never realize the destination as a harbor for a great national continental railroad transportation heretofore adverted to would seem to prophesy as the future of a properly located and constructed harbor.

THE REASONS OF THE SOUTHERN PACIFIC COMPANY FOR BUILDING ITS SANTA MONICA WHARF

The fact that the Southern Pacific Company has expended a large amount of money in acquiring its present holdings at Port Los Angeles is dwelt on at some length in arguments and in documents filed with this Board as some evidence of the fact that, in the opinion of this corporation, that location is the best upon this coast for a harbor.

My acquaintance with transportation conditions upon this coast leads me to believe that its actions in that respect are entitled to no such weight, and I think that a simple statement of the facts will demonstrate this.

Testimony has been submitted to the Board of the large commerce done at San Pedro when that was the only port for the city of Los Angeles. It has also been shown that that commerce, excepting as to certain articles handled by vessels which enter the inner harbor, has largely fallen off within the past few years.

I have already adverted to the construction of the wharf at Redondo and its connection with the city of Los Angeles by two lines of railway. It is a fact that at present the principal maritime commerce of this coast is between this city and San Francisco and way points.

The Redondo Wharf after it was open for commerce took from San Pedro about 62 per cent of this coast commerce to and from San Francisco. For reasons I have explained it also secured the larger part of the commerce brought to this part of the coast in deep-draft vessels around the Horn.

The entrance of the Los Angeles Terminal Railway into San Pedro in 1891 would divide with the Southern Pacific Company what remained of the coast commerce at that port. The Southern Pacific Company thus found itself suffering a loss of considerably more than half of the commerce which it had originally enjoyed at San Pedro, and threatened with a loss of more.

By building its pier at Santa Monica that company has returned upon the Redondo people the trick which they served upon it with reference to the commerce in the direction of San Francisco, and it has at the same time continued its competition with the Los Angeles Terminal Railway at San Pedro for the important business which continues to come to that port. It has also the further advantage in the location of its Santa Monica Wharf that no wharf can be built westward of Port Los Angeles for the reason that the topography of the country is such that no line of railway can ever reach Los Angeles beyond that point, and it will there always have the first and last call on commerce to and from San Francisco. Furthermore, no other railroad company was likely to go to the large expense of building into that place and expending something like $1,000,000 in the construction of the costly wharf necessary to do business there for the purpose of merely dividing with the Southern Pacific Company the coast commerce which the location at that point attracts.

By building its pier at that place the Southern Pacific Company also secured a method of landing the immense quantities of coal which it uses upon its southern system, directly from the ship to the bunkers, instead of lightering it as it had theretofore done at San Pedro, and also has provided a place where deep-draft vessels can unload their cargoes directly from the ship to the cars, an advantage enjoyed only by Redondo until the building of the wharf at Port Los Angeles. The advantages which the Southern Pacific Company thus gained, and will always retain, for handling the largest portion of the coast commerce in the direction of San Francisco, of which commerce will of course increase greatly in the future, and in handling its coal, will amply repay it for the investment which it has made at Santa Monica without reference to the utilization of that port for the character of commerce intended to be accommodated by the harbor which it is proposed by the Government to construct on this coast. In addition to that, the possibility of using its Santa Monica improvements as a means of diverting the construction of the deep-water harbor from San Pedro, where it has to meet competing conditions, to Santa Monica, where it has superior rights which can never be overcome, was certainly worth a good deal.

In this connection I desire to quote to the Board from the speech made by Senator Perkins in the United States Senate, when the bill carrying the appropriation for this deep-water harbor, and providing for this Board, was under discussion. It may not be improper as an introduction to this to say that Senator Perkins came to this coast some forty-five years ago, as a sailor before the mast, and since that time he has had maintained an intimate acquaintance with the coast of California, first as a sailor and afterwards as a shipowner, and he is to-day a member of a firm owning the most extensive line of vessels plying upon this coast.

Senator Perkins says [speaking of the Southern Pacific Company]:

"They never seriously intended building a wharf outside [meaning the outer harbor at San Pedro] until the breakwater was completed, because they had ample facilities inside for the transportation of all the freight that came there. The great objection to it was lighterage. It was one of the great expenses that ships having

a heavy draft of water, more than 18 feet, could not go in over the bar at Wilmington, and the result was that the ships were obliged to anchor in San Pedro roadstead and there lighter their coal on shore. So there was a rival wharf built at a place called Redondo on the southern portion of Santa Monica Bay, and that wharf was getting a large amount of business that came from the north, because passengers and freight would reach Los Angeles City via Redondo several hours before they could on vessels coming from the north going via San Pedro. It was a wise business undertaking, and it is characteristic of the enterprise and sagacity and business foresight of the management of that great railroad company. As I have said before, for his enterprise, for his energy, for his push, Mr. Huntington is the peer of any man in this country. So he wisely said, 'We will build a wharf on this bay where we can save this lighterage.' Do you know that they use from 10,000 to 15,000 tons of coal per month that is obliged to go over their road to various distribution depots? So the railroad company decided to build this wharf at Santa Monica and save this dollar a ton lighterage which was paid to another company. It was a wise business enterprise. It was not an experiment. * * * The wharf at Santa Monica, as I have said, has been a good business investment. I believe the saving alone to the Southern Pacific upon its lighterage of coal and lumber and other supplies will amount to not less than $15,000 and perhaps $20,000 per month, and by reason of their facilities for doing other business, for handling merchandise coming in over the wharves from other countries, as well as our own coast States, they can handle it much more cheaply than anybody else can, and this will correspondingly add to their revenue. Therefore the building of this wharf is a splendid business investment, and I do not believe that the projectors of the wharf when they built it had any expectation of asking the Government to build a breakwater."

I don't know of a person in California who, from his own intimate acquaintance with transportation matters upon this coast, is more competent to speak upon this point than is the Senator just quoted, and it would seem that what he says is so reasonable that it should dispose of the claim which I have just been discussing.

Before passing this point it may be appropriate to notice the claims advanced by the advocates of the location at Port Los Angeles, founded upon the alleged greater nearness of that point to Los Angeles. A great deal has been made of this difference between Los Angeles and that point and San Pedro.

In a report which I have in my hand, issued by the Government, of a hearing had before the House Committee on Rivers and Harbors, on February 28, 1896, of engineers advocating the superior advantages of Port Los Angeles for a deep-water harbor, Mr. Corthell is made to state: "Southern California, of which the city of Los Angeles is the center of population and trade, has increased in population, and similarly in all other directions, about 350 per cent in the last fifteen years, and Los Angeles is only 12 miles from Port Los Angeles, where it is proposed to build the breakwater and make a protected harbor."

I am under the impression that this document has been submitted to the Board, and I know that in the matter which has been submitted to it are statements with reference to relative distances between the city of Los Angeles and Port Los Angeles and San Pedro.

I will file with the Board a time and distance table for the Los Angeles division of the Southern Pacific Railroad system, by which it operates its trains, which will show that the distance between Los Angeles and San Pedro is placed at 22.10 miles; between Los Angeles and Port Los Angeles, at 20.40 miles, being a difference in favor of Port Los Angeles of 1.70 miles, which difference would probably be increased a matter of 2 miles on all trains running from piers that might be constructed in the proposed outer harbor at San Pedro—a difference, it is unnecessary for me to say, so trifling as not to be considered in railroad transportation, and especially, as in this case, where it is more than compensated for by grades largely in favor of San Pedro, as has been shown by the testimony of Mr. Hawgood.

There is also, it appears to me, another objection to the location of the harbor at Port Los Angeles and which may in its ultimate results seriously impair the usefulness of any harbor located there.

The Board will note that the map submitted to them shows that the narrow beach approach to Port Los Angeles extends for a considerable distance in front of the town of Santa Monica. This is an incorporated city, and, under the laws of the State of California, no railroad can be constructed within the limits of a municipality in this State without the consent of its board of trustees or city council. It is quite within the power of the legislative body of that city to prohibit the widening of the approach to Port Los Angeles to more than the 50 feet now already held there by the Southern Pacific Company, should that body deem a further occupancy of its beach by railroads detrimental to the interests of the city. Indeed, if the present franchise of the Southern Pacific along its right of way fronting that town calls for a definite number of tracks as one or two, that number can not be increased without the consent of the board of trustees of the city of Santa Monica.

The importance of this place has arisen from its being a very charming seaside resort, and largely the favorite resort of that kind for the citizens of Los Angeles and the surrounding country. It doesn't seem to me improbable to presume that the citizens of that town will soon find that the attractiveness of its beach, to which it is indebted for its prosperity and present importance, will be seriously impaired by any extension of the railroad use of the same. If that should come to be generally felt in that city it is hardly probable that any other line of railroad will be built there without infinite trouble, if at all. Certainly under the laws as they exist in this State the use of the proposed harbor for commerce, except what can be carried over the present lines of the Southern Pacific aligning the water front of the town, will be absolutely at the mercy of the board of trustees of a seaside village, a condition of affairs of sufficient gravity to have induced Senator White to speak very earnestly about the matter, as will be shown by a perusal of his speech on the harbor question, filed with this Board, which it seems to me would hardly encourage a large expenditure of Government funds at that place.

COMPARATIVE ADVANTAGES OF SAN PEDRO.

From the point of view of a railway company the advantages shown to be lacking at Santa Monica exist in full measure at San Pedro, and is comparatively free from the disadvantages noted at Santa Monica.

Just here, with the indulgence of the Board, I desire to say a word as to what appears to me to be very plainly an error made by Mr. Corthell in his address to you upon last Monday in construing the force and effect of the law providing for the improvement of the inner harbor at San Pedro. After quoting certain extracts from the speech of Senator Frye, and a letter in his possession, Mr. Corthell states as his conclusion: "That is, Congress was unwilling to do any more work at Wilmington on the inner harbor if the outer harbor should be built at San Pedro, and facilities therefor for local commerce requiring deeper water than the present work has provided—13½ feet at low water—must be established in the outer harbor; in other words, they must abandon the inner harbor and move out."

The law from which Mr. Corthell deduced that conclusion reads as follows:

"For improving Wilmington Harbor, California, in accordance with the project submitted February 7, 1895, $50,000: Provided, That contracts may be entered into by the Secretary of War for such materials and work as may be necessary to complete said project, to be paid for as appropriations may from time to time be made by law, not to exceed in the aggregate $342,000, exclusive of the amount herein appropriated [$50,000]; but no such contracts shall be entered into until the Board provided for in this act to determine the location of a deep-water harbor for commerce and of refugees between Port Los Angeles in Santa Monica Bay and San Pedro, in the State of California, has made its report to the Secretary of War, and not at all if said report shall be in favor of San Pedro as the location of said harbor."

The project referred to in that law as "the project submitted February 7, 1895," is the project of Colonel Benyaurd for the attainment of 4 feet additional depth at the entrance to the inner harbor. (Ex. Doc. No. 61, Fifty-third Congress, copies of which I believe have been filed with this Board.)

How it is possible to have deduced from the wording of this law any hostility of Congress to the inner harbor at San Pedro; any expression of unwillingness to do any more work at Wilmington in the inner harbor; any notice that the inner harbor must be abandoned and its occupants move out, is something which I have been unable to comprehend.

The appropriation to begin work remains undisturbed. It is an appropriation which can not be spent for the maintenance or other expenses of the harbor, but must be spent for commencing and prosecuting, as far as the same will go, the work on the inner harbor recommended in the project of Colonel Benyaurd. It is, I submit, as plain a commitment of the Government to that work as a whole as can be made in words.

The simple fact is that the location of the deep-water harbor at San Pedro will, by the terms of the law, have the effect of taking what shall remain to be done of the work upon Colonel Benyaurd's project, after the $50,000 shall have been expended, out of the continuing-contract system under which it would otherwise remain and placing it under the annual appropriation system.

The reason for this change and the way in which it came to be made amply sustain this view of the law, if any support were needed.

Since Mr. Corthell, in support of his opinion, referred to his recollection of the facts concerning this matter, I trust that I may be permitted to advert to certain of them with which I happen to be personally acquainted on account of having been present at Washington when the legislation in question was had.

The clause for the improvement of the inner harbor at San Pedro, above quoted,

without, however, that part providing for the possible lapsing of the $342,000 continuing-contract provision, was adopted by the Senate as an amendment to the river and harbor act as it came from the House, and was in the act in that form when the bill was sent to the conference committee. That part of the bill appropriating nearly $3,000,000 for the deep-sea harbor was also added as a Senate amendment. When the matter came up for consideration in the conference committee the clause relating to the appropriation for the inner harbor was amended by the addition thereto of the words, "but no such contracts shall be entered into until the Board provided for in this act to determine the location of a deep-water harbor for commerce and of refuge, as between Port Los Angeles in Santa Monica Bay and San Pedro, in the State of California, has made its report to the Secretary of War, and not at all if said report shall be in favor of San Pedro as the location of said harbor." In addition to that, at the time the change was made by adding the words just quoted, I was informed by Senator White, of California, that in considering the matter the conference committee were of the opinion that in view of the large amount carried by the river and harbor bill, being as it was about $60,000,000—one of the largest river and harbor bills ever passed by Congress—and the depleted condition of the Treasury, it was thought that if it should be decided to spend the larger appropriation at San Pedro the presence in the bill of the whole appropriation of $392,000 for the inner harbor, would appear to constitute, when taken together, too large a sum to be given to one place. It was therefore provided that in the event of the expenditure of the larger sum at San Pedro the work upon the inner harbor project not paid for by the $50,000 should be taken off the continuing-contract system and left to be prosecuted by future appropriations as Congress should decide.

In view of this, it would appear that the entertainment of any anxiety as to the existence of a possible sentiment of opposition in Congress toward San Pedro's inner harbor, and especially the anticipation that the tenants of that harbor are in danger of being served with a notice from the Government to move out, is an entirely uncalled for exercise of sympathetic anticipation.

The blue print filed with this Board by Mr. Hawgood, with the intention of showing the ownership of the water front upon the westerly side of the inner and proposed deep-water harbor at San Pedro, was made up from data collected from the public records of the county, and its correctness can be fully demonstrated if there is any disposition upon the part of anyone to question it. It shows such a diversity of ownership of the frontage of the inner harbor as to demonstrate beyond a question the absolute impossibility of any monopoly of its advantages, not counting the fact that the eastern water front of the inner harbor is also subject to other ownership. It will be noted that by that map the Southern Pacific Company is shown to own a considerable strip of land aligning that portion of the proposed outer harbor from which wharves can be most easily projected.

It has been claimed here that the Southern Pacific holdings on the water front of the proposed deep-water harbor at San Pedro tend to give that company a monopoly of its advantages. I think the inspection which this Board has already made of that location has probably shown you that the topography of the country west of that Southern Pacific holdings, is such as not to offer any serious difficulties of approach by any other railway company that may desire to reach the harbor front by crossing the Southern Pacific track.

The mesa or high plain lying west of the proposed deep-water harbor and under the Palos Verdes Hill also affords several hundred acres of ground excellently adapted to the construction of warehouses and storage depots for any commerce which it may be necessary to handle to and from the deep-water harbor. As to the inner harbor, the opportunity afforded to shippers for securing these apparently necessary adjuncts to the commerce of a large seaport is practically unlimited.

In addition to that, another advantage, entirely lacking at Santa Monica, and as to whose necessity in connection with such a harbor as it is desired to secure there can, it seems to me, be no two opinions, exists in perfect form at San Pedro. I mean the opportunity for docks and interior basins where ships may be placed for cleaning and repairing. The 18 feet of water over the bar at the present time would enable almost any vessel to go into the inner harbor after her cargo was discharged, and when that depth is increased to 22 feet by the completion of the Benyaurd project, there would appear no reason why any ship of commerce which sails the ocean might not find inside all such accommodations for dockage and repair as could be needed after the longest or hardest voyage.

Reference has been made in what I have quoted from the report of the Board of 1892, and also in quotations which have been made to the Board from Senator Frye's speech, to the relation which the proposed harbor will sustain to the commerce coming through the Nicaragua Canal when that enterprise shall have been completed, as it is confidently hoped and believed through all the western portion of the

By 1973 landslides and fill had obliterated all evidence of the existence of Port Los Angeles. Shortly after this photograph was made, the lighthouse that was located at the site from which Port Los Angeles extended out to sea was torn down. One wonders what this view would be today if Collis P. Huntington had been successful in his attempt to make Santa Monica the main port for Los Angeles. Possibly Santa Monica Canyon would be filled with warehouses and tracks, and the view of the bay blocked by long wharves and docked and moving ships.

142

Index

PAMPHLETS

Corthell, E. L. *Santa Monica, a Protected Harbor.* Santa Monica, Press of the Outlook, 1894.

Cowick, Kate L. *The Outlook's Story of Santa Monica.* Santa Monica, The Evening Outlook, 1932.

Goodrich, Ernest Payson. *Report to Harbor Commission of Los Angeles Concerning the Development and Construction of an Ocean Harbor.* Reprinted. Los Angeles, Los Angeles Examiner, n.d.

Swett, Ira, ed. *Lines of Pacific Electric — Western District.* Los Angeles, Interurbans, 1957.

PUBLIC DOCUMENTS

U.S. Congress. House. *U.S. Engineering Department Report on Deep Water Harbor at San Pedro Bay.* House Ex. Doc. No. 41, 52nd Cong., 2nd sess., 1892.

U.S. Congress. Senate. *Report of a Hearing Before the Committee on Commerce on the Subject of a Deep Water Harbor in Southern California.* Washington, D.C.: Government Printing Office, 1896.

U.S. Congress. Senate. *Deep Water Harbor at Port Los Angeles or at San Pedro, California.* (Walker Board Report) S. Doc. 18, 55th Cong., 1st sess., 1897.

REPORTS

Deep Water Harbor in Southern California, Port Los Angeles vs San Pedro. Report of oral testimony at Public Hearing in Los Angeles, December, 1896. Los Angeles, Evening Express Company, n.d.

Natural Advantages of Redondo Beach for the Accommodation of Deep-Sea Commerce. Reports from Col. G. H. Mendell (Corps of Eng., U.S. Army) and William Hamilton Hall (State Eng. of Calif.) transmitted to the Board of Trade of Los Angeles. San Francisco, H. S. Crocker Co., 1888.